"Janet Thomas is one of the most inspiring people I've met. Lemons, Lemonade & Life allows readers to put her sage advice into action. Everyone can benefit from reading this book and following the exercises she outlines. You will live a saner, happier life if you do." —Jane Greenstein

"Congratulations to Janet Thomas for this very personal, honest, heartfelt revelation. Lemons, Lemonade & Life is a fresh, insightful and creative recipe for personal growth, change and transformation." —Oscar DeGruy

"Janet Thomas is one of the brightest and most insightful women. She is truly an inspiration. I found her book to be invaluable in its content. It will provide anyone going through a difficult time with the tools they need to better their life." —Said Ghazanfar

"My thoughts and feelings about Lemons, Lemonade & Life are simple. It works and helps. It truly did that for me. I did the exercises while reading it and it took me way back to my childhood and brought up memories that I had forgotten. It was an amazing experience and by following the instructions it was easy to get there, which I really appreciate. I know for a fact this book (and the ones that will follow) will help others as well." —Nicky Sandels

"Finally, a book that not only has information, but actual processes that will make your life work much better. Do them and start feeling happy again!"—Peter D., age 76

"Janet helps you pick up the pieces and move through and past the pain when life has handed you lemons. The book provides powerful processes and sweet inspiration. It is a recipe book for transforming life's sour lemons into delicious lemonade. Her recipes work whether the pain is lingering from the past or comes from a more recent challenge."—Robin Quinn, Spiritual Coach, Los Angeles

"Eureka! Finally, a tool that teaches us how to process our emotions. Lemons, Lemonade & Life's profound methods are groundbreaking, easy to read and can be gently comprehended. Once read and practiced, then we can share with others how to process our feelings and emotions to make this world a better place with less wounded beings." —Veda Adams, MBA, Nutritionist & Peace Activist

"In a world full of overstressed, overstimulated, overmedicated and undernourished souls, this book is the answer. It provides simple tools to facilitate a vacation from the hamster wheel, if even for just a few minutes a day. This book improved my mental and physical well-being and has enabled me to live a more fulfilling, uncomplicated life."—Amanda W., Recovering Worrier and Insomniac

"At last! A doable, effective and practical guide to work out the bugs in your life."—Lillian Decoud

"Janet has used her life experiences to create a unique guide to self-awareness and self-realization that will benefit all who read it."—Joyce Smith

"A truly authentic work, carefully crafted and brilliantly written. Thomas goes far beyond providing a self-help guide to those desiring to escape from past or present injuries. She gives us a profound wake-up call that reminds us all of our inherent power and inner strength to overcome whatever obstacles or difficulties we may encounter in life."—Dr. Joy A. DeGruy, Author and Social Scientist

"Ever had a lemon seed get stuck in your straw and stop the flow? I have. After reading Janet's unique insight into solving life's problems in Lemons, Lemonade & Life, I am able to get 'un-stuck.' Thanks, Janet, for helping me to go with the flow."—Mary Ellen Woods-Iler

"I don't know much about metaphysics or anything of the sort, but I do know that my mom is the strongest, most inspirational woman I could ever be lucky enough to know. She has taught me that I have a choice in how I can view situations in my life that are within and without my control, and I am infinitely better off for it." —Aaron Thomas

When the going gets tough,
the tough ... make lemonade

At least that's what author Janet Thomas did. She had her share of life's lemons, from sexual abuse to clinical depression to obesity and beyond. She could have just decided to pitch her tent in the citrus section of life's grocery store and succumbed to the sour — but she didn't. Instead she turned her life around, then examined what she learned and turned to help others. The power of Janet's presence in these written words awakens and energizes your inherent desire to love and lift yourself.

Using the metaphor of making lemonade, *Lemons, Lemonade & Life* gently guides you through a unique process of discovering:

   ...*what* it is you want

   ...*why* you don't yet have it, and, most importantly

   ...*how* you can turn those things you currently perceive as anchors dragging you down into resources for launching yourself upward.

Whatever your challenges, *Lemons, Lemonade & Life* uniquely inspires and encourages healing and wholeness. Anything you find as a block can be addressed and transformed using Janet's positive, self-supportive approach. As her words, thoughts, and techniques kindle the flame of confidence deep within, you will find yourself:

- Improving your physical health
- Releasing yourself from addiction
- Dropping unwanted weight
- Discovering how to develop your natural gifts and talents
- Seeing things you have constantly struggled with disappear with ease
- Attracting new friends
- Enjoying healthier relationships
- Gaining the ability to attract abundance into your life
- and much, much more.

Many books are useful because they present familiar ideas in a different way. This book is invaluable because it demonstrates looking at *life* in a different way. No matter what lemons you may have been given, this is the key for using them as key ingredients for finding your true, best self and restoring sweetness to your experience of life every day.

Lemons, Lemonade & Life

Lemons, Lemonade & Life

Practical Steps for Getting the Sweetness Back
When Life Goes Sour

Janet D. Thomas

Healing Soldier Publishing

Sherman Oaks, California

Printed in the United States of America

Library of Congress Control Number: 2011916666

ISBN: 978-0-9840264-6-3

Book Consultant: Ellen Reid
Book Cover & Interior Design: Ghislain Viau
Editor: Robin Quinn

To the Dreamers,
Light Workers and Pioneers

Contents

Acknowledgements   xv

Introduction   xix

Let's Go!   1
    Honor, Clarity and Abundance   5
    Preliminaries   8
    Preparation   8
        Utensil #1: Your Dreams   9
        Utensil #2: Going "Offline"   10
        Utensil #3: Writing   11
        Idea #1: Neutralization   14
        Idea #2: About Your Thoughts   24
        Idea #3: About Your Emotions   25
    Pep Talk #1   27

Lemons   31
    Definition   31
    Lemons — A Closer Look   35
    Lemons — Your Blueprint for Success   39

Water   43
    Listening   45
    Releasing Emotion   53

Time to Add Water   60
Using Your Imagination   69
The Anger Release Exercise   71
Transform Your B, S, G and R   80
The Guilt/Regret Exercise   85
Pep Talk #2   88

Sugar   91

To Have and To Hold   91
Perception: Your Ultimate Freedom   94
A Puzzle for Game Lovers   99
Puzzle #2 – More Information   102
Love: The Final Frontier   105
Love: Fill in the Gaps   108
Unconditional Love: It's All Yours!   111
Pep Talk #3   124
The Dirty Backpack Exercise   129

Afterword   131

About the Author   133

Acknowledgements

To Ellen Reid, master book shepherd, I extend my humble appreciation. It is because of your generosity of spirit and commitment to excellence that my manuscript is in book form today. Thank you for your friendship and support.

Robin Quinn, your editing magic gave my manuscript the polish it needed. Thank you for your talent, guidance and words of support. I am very grateful.

To Laren Bright, wordsmith extraordinaire, and Ghislain Viau, dazzling creative designer, your talents built the pillars on which I stand to be of service. Thank you.

To Starla Fortunado, you are a brilliant photographer! Thanks to you, Kurumi Uchino and Dino Parenti, for helping to attract those who may be interested in what I have to share.

Heartfelt thanks to all service-oriented beings for your love and dedication. To self-help authors, philosophers and lovers of mankind, I am a product of you. I am animating *your* messages and thank you so much for the gifts of guidance. Specifically, to the following authors, your books helped me so much during my journey to wellness: Jane Roberts, Louise Hay, Marianne Williamson, Wayne Dyer, John Bradshaw, Julia Cameron, Barbara DeAngelis, Shakti Gawain, Elisabeth Kubler-Ross, Dan Millman, Deepak Chopra and M. Scott Peck.

To Liliana Sterling and her parents, Bill and Theresa; to my extended family and wonderful family of friends, including Nana, Grandpa, Nikki, Jordan, Vickie and Margaret, and more angels than I can count, thank you for your love and support.

To my hands-on teachers and guides, Susan S. O'Hara, LCSW, BCD, Shawn Randall and Darryl Anka, thank you for being the light in the tunnel. To Maurice Rapkin, PhD, your anger release expertise, your love and kindness emanates throughout these words.

To Auntie Joyce, Veda Adams, Laurie Boyer, LMFT, Dolores Chappelle, Dr. Joy DeGruy, Oscar DeGruy, Dr. Julie Foster, Said N. Ghazanfar, Jane Greenstein, Miatta Mansion, Tara Marshall, Nicky Sandels, Robin Southers, Dr. Ian Thompson and Amanda Wilson, please accept my gratitude for providing feedback on my draft manuscript. I love and respect you so much, and thank you for your support and encouragement.

To Butch and Mary Ellen Woods-Iler, thank you. Mary Ellen, thank you for your friendship, and for your humor, words (and silences) of wisdom.

To all of my sisters, I cherish you! How lucky I am to be surrounded by such awesome cheerleaders, my goodness!

To my brothers, Steven and Daniel, and to Fred, you are brilliant men, loving fathers and loyal friends. I love and respect you more than you know.

To my parents, Peter and Lillian, you provide me with stability, humor and love. You have always been ahead of your time in your thinking. I love being your daughter and am grateful to call you my best friends.

To everyone who loves Aaron, I love you!

And, finally, to Aaron. My heart reawakened when you were born, and with my every breath, throughout (and beyond) time and space, I will honor you.

Introduction

I must have started drafting this introduction at least ten times. I thought about telling you my background (born to working-class parents, grew up in Inglewood, California, survivor of childhood sexual abuse, hard-working corporate gal, mother, channel and medium). I thought about providing suggestions on how to use this guide (it's a quick read, then go back and work it slowly if you're so inclined ... take what you can use and know that it will work if you have the courage and commitment to work it ... be prepared for your life to sweeten up quite a bit without anything in it changing at first but you). I also thought about sharing my experiences to let you know that I have some credibility when it comes to talking about healing (overcame life experiences that also included obesity, clinical depression, chronic shoplifting, compulsive lying, low self-esteem, divorce, bankruptcy, eviction and rape). I even thought about discussing my beliefs (that you can live an amazingly rewarding life from where you are *right now* ... that your life is a perfect reflection of your inner world ... that you are loved beyond belief and to learn to get out of your own way in order to perceive it). Finally, I also thought about writing on why my how-to guide is different than others (for this, I have no clue). Somehow none of these approaches felt right to me.

I remember when I was little, I constantly fantasized about being rich and famous ... about living in a big, beautiful house and having people gush all over me, telling me how beautiful, brilliant, smart, funny and talented I was. I cannot tell you how many speeches I made in my head upon being crowned Miss America, or how many Grammys and Oscars I have won, how many rich and gorgeous men were competing with each other for the privilege of marrying me, or how I was hailed as a hero for patenting inventions that would help heal the world.

And frankly, as I now find myself in a place of peace and inner joy, none of that matters to me anymore. I am not interested in people gushing all over me, and I am only interested in talking about myself to the extent that it may assist someone else, for what unites us is that we are *all* survivors in some way. Candidly, I am really preoccupied with being of service. The only thing I really want to do is gush all over *you*; to reflect how courageous, smart, funny, talented and amazing *you* are! I believe that you are sacred and so completely deserving of love. If you think that unbelievable and incredibly corny, wait 'til you apply some of the ideas I talk about, do the exercises in this book, and garner a deeper appreciation for yourself. Then perhaps you'll understand where I'm coming from.

My son described me as being a "soldier" in a Mother's Day letter he wrote to me when he was a senior in high school. Not only did it never occur to me that he would ever perceive me as such, given my gentle cheerleading nature, I also didn't give him the credit he deserved for being as intuitive as he was (and is). For, in truth, I'm nothing if not passionate in my obsession to love and support others as strongly and as fully as I can, and I also no longer take issue with the camouflaged intensity with which I live my life, having lived in dogged determination to heal from my own arsenal of challenging experiences and situations while continuing to go to work each day to support my family. So the puzzle pieces that fit for me, based upon my journey thus far, do equate to me being a healing soldier.

Who knows what tomorrow holds. For now, it is my intention to infuse as much corny and gushy love into the planet (and to you) that I can muster (and that you are willing to receive). I invite you to come play and dance with me within the wonder of and gratitude for your own beingness. To overwhelm the gloom and to laugh until we all have six-pack abs on the inside even if we're morbidly obese. For who cares what we really look like or where we come from or what we believe *while* we radiate love, as long as we *are* radiating love? And our ability to radiate love starts from within.

Come with me …

Let's Go!

Making lemonade is pretty simple. Lemons are very tart when eaten plain. However, when you add water and sugar to dilute them, they are downright delicious!

Lemonade is the signature summer drink. On a hot day, it quenches our thirst and gives us energy. In fall and winter, drinking it can remind us of summertime. Lemons are also healthy for the body, and they bring out the flavor in food. I love lemonade, good food, and feeling great, therefore I love lemons.

You probably have already heard the cliché, *"When life gives you lemons, make lemonade."* I believe we hear it so often because it's such a wonderful and useful saying. So let's start there.

I've heard stories of people overcoming some amazing circumstances. Leonardo Del Vecchio, founder of one of the world's largest designers and manufacturers of sunglasses and prescription eyewear, was one of five children, and he was raised in an orphanage after his widowed mother couldn't support him. To date, he has amassed a fortune worth billions of dollars.

Carly Simon used to stutter as a child. Working with her mother's suggestion to sing her words, Carly overcame her stuttering issue, and she is now celebrated by generations for her beautiful voice and musical artistry.

Frederick Douglass was born into slavery, survived his circumstances and escaped, and then went on to become a celebrated public speaker and writer. As part of his life's work, he fought for justice, women's rights and equal opportunity.

Finally, look at Oprah. Born to a teenage mother and herself a survivor of childhood sexual abuse, Oprah is known worldwide by her first name.

Each of them made serious lemonade out of some serious lemons and enjoyed amazing realities. And throughout the ages, countless and nameless others have done it as well, which lets me know that it is absolutely possible to do. The path is already paved.

Thinking about such successful people is how I made the connection. I told myself, *"It is possible to unveil your talents and passions and make your dreams come true. Others have successfully done it, and from pretty nasty beginnings at that. If they can do it, then why can't I do it too?"*

I used to think, "Sorry, but folks like Leonardo Del Vecchio and Oprah are special." I believed that successful folks were born with superior abilities and characteristics that I didn't have. Some people just seemed to have that Midas touch. I knew that I wasn't one of them. But the thought of making lemonade out of lemons still intrigued me because I was always a dreamer. Even during rough times, I imagined what my life would be like if I could manifest fun, love, happiness, harmony and abundance.

I guess a stubborn nature can come in handy from time to time because I constantly explored ideas and techniques that would unlock the door leading to a path of joy, success and fulfillment. Although my dreams did not include wanting to be a billionaire, I sure wanted to convert what I felt was a cursed life into a blissful one. To be honest, I am obsessed with finding and using tools and techniques that convert pain into joy. More than thirty years have passed since I made that initial intention to transform my life, and the journey continues to be remarkable.

I can now proudly say that I am a true lemonade maker, and from there have manifested amazing things into my life. And I might add that it turns out to be a wonderful way of life. For many years, I didn't think it was possible for me to live happily given my lemons, but I am living proof that it is possible. Life has become very, very sweet indeed!

I have learned to make lemonade as follows:

- Lemons: Traumatizing and/or difficult life circumstances
- Water: Acknowledging and expressing the impact of these experiences
- Sugar: Gaining clarity and strength from them and putting them to work on my behalf

I have found this recipe to be extremely effective and rewarding, and I will explore it with you.

This is what is possible when you learn how to make lemonade this way. You can:

- Improve your physical health
- Release yourself from addiction
- Be able to develop your natural gifts and talents
- See the things that you have constantly struggled with now disappear with ease
- Attract new friends
- Enjoy healthier relationships
- Gain the ability to attract abundance into your life
- And much more!

At times, I've wondered, *"If it's possible to have it all, then why can't we all have it? Why can't we all live the life of our dreams? If someone else can create what they want, why can't we?"* And why not *you?* Well, I say that we can. And YOU can, from where you are, right now. It's time to move into a different future, starting today!

ᄋᄋ ᄋᄋ ᄋᄋ

Honor, Clarity and Abundance

When you learn how to make lemonade out of lemons, you may discover that it has far-reaching implications. You actually learn *to honor who you are,* which paves the way to creating the reality you desire. When you feel, *really* feel, just a slight tinge of honoring yourself for a split second, it will rock your world and you'll be forever changed. This is exciting and true!

Honor is defined as:

- *Showing a courteous regard for,* and
- *Holding in high respect.*

Imagine some wonderful things that you dream about being, such as being happy and being loved. Or think about some of the things that you dream about having, such as abundance or new experiences.

What do you dream about being able to do? Do you dream about going on a vacation? Or being able to kick your boss to the curb because you're successful doing your own thing? Do you envision doing artwork, moving into another career of your dreams, or excelling at the one you're in now? Imagine all of the things that you want.

Now imagine yourself having a courteous regard for yourself, and holding yourself in high respect *first, while* you pursue your dreams. The feeling is way more amazing than anything you can imagine, and your journey becomes more exciting and immensely joyful. That is what making lemonade out of lemons will allow you to experience.

Also, when you learn to make lemonade out of lemons, you gain *clarity*. Looking more closely, *clarity* is defined as:

- *Freedom from indistinctness or ambiguity, and*
- *Clearness or lucidity as to perception or understanding.*

Notice the basic meaning behind each definition: *free* and *clear*. *Imagine that*! You will gradually and softly grow to be clear about *what* you know *when* you know it. You will not disown it, you will accept it. You will recapture your sound judgment. You will more easily identify who has your back and who does not. You will trust that every move you make is in the right direction. *Free* and *clear*: you learn to trust yourself again.

It is worth repeating that when you learn to make lemonade out of lemons, you can attract *abundance*. Are you really clear about what abundance is? So often we think that abundance only means having a lot of money. Having a lot of money qualifies as one definition of abundance but why limit the definition to just that one? Here are a few more definitions for abundance:

- *An extremely plentiful or overly sufficient quantity or supply*
- *Overflowing fullness, and*
- *The ability to do what you want to do when you want to do it.*

Each definition invites you to expand your view of abundance. By doing so, you can attract more of it into your life and also see ways that you're already abundant. You may already have an abundance of friends, an abundance of love, an abundance of laughter, and/or an abundance of hope. However, you might not see it as abundance because of your narrow definition of the word.

What if you could have something that you really want quickly without having to wait for the money? Would you be open to receiving this if it were a gift, or would you rather wait for the money? Now do a quick status check: ask yourself if you're willing to expand your ideas about what abundance is, and if you are, think about the ways in which you're already abundant.

The point here (and forevermore!) is to be willing to expand your thinking and to be open to embrace new ideas.

CR CR CR

Preliminaries

To help you make lemonade (a mixture of lemons, water and sugar), I will provide simple, gentle and effective tools on *how* to do it. My goal is to share some ideas that can assist you to create the life you want to live.

In each section, there will be information for you to consider, along with different perspectives to try on for size. *You* are the ultimate decision-maker when it comes to your life — on what works and what doesn't. So take from this only what you truly think you can use.

With *Lemons, Lemonade & Life*, I want to let you know that you're supported ... that there is a way to break through some things that may be holding you back. You can uncover, acknowledge and use your special gifts and talents. You can transform your thinking from "I *should* love myself" to actually having a level of self-respect, clarity and self-love that is unquestionable and is embedded into your very being. And from there, you can create a life full of miracles, love and joy.

With those intentions, here is my offering to you.

CR CR CR

Preparation

To make lemonade in the kitchen, perhaps you would use a knife, lemon squeezer and a spoon. To make lemonade from the lemons in your life, you will need some utensils as well, and they are: (1) Your Dreams, (2) Going "Offline," and (3) Writing.

Utensil #1: Your Dreams

Before you begin to make lemonade, it's a good idea to prepare for what you want. You may already be quite clear about what your lemons are, which is exciting because you have good stuff to play with and transform. And while you transform your lemons, what will your lemonade look like in its place?

It's time to use your imagination. Open up your mind and daydream a bit. Once you develop the skill of learning how to make lemonade out of lemons, what will your version of lemonade look like? Seriously, what do *YOU* want? Take everyone else out of the picture and think about what it is that *you* want to attract into your life.

Do you dream about supporting your family? Selling your artwork? Having a wonderful marriage? Enjoying a home filled with family, friendship, laughter and love? Losing weight or quitting smoking? Having a terrific career? Being a great parent?

Now is the time to start thinking about things that make you smile on the inside and make your heart beat a little faster. Incorporate your dreams into your daily life. You can make the possibilities of them come alive simply by thinking about them and feeling good about them.

Utensil #2: Going "Offline"

Television, the Internet and cell phones are wonderful tools. They entertain us, help us research and explore whatever appeals to us, keep us in touch with those we love, and allow us to communicate, world-wide, in a matter of moments. They are also perfect distractions. There is one thing you won't find on the Internet — *yourself.*

While making lemonade, be willing to go "offline." This means signing off of the Internet, turning off the TV, and putting your phone on silent. Put aside the bills or laundry and your other daily life tasks for at least *fifteen minutes* each day. All of the things you busy yourself with in your life are terrific, however you can give yourself permission to take a break from them. Fifteen minutes of *"you* time" is the minimum (which can easily be disguised as a bathroom break if you lack privacy right now).

Imagine that your life is just like a movie (it doesn't matter whether you would consider it a romantic comedy, an action-adventure, horror or dramatic film). Imagine that you're sitting in a movie theater watching your life unfolding on the big screen. Now, when you go offline for fifteen minutes, it's as if you're going to the theater lobby for a breather or for more popcorn.

It's always great to have understanding and supportive people around you who you can talk to and share with.

Continue to enjoy that. If you can find someone who you trust (whether it be a friend, family member, co-worker, or others) to talk with about this information that would be terrific. However, you might find that you can attract the things you want in your life more quickly by incorporating offline time just for yourself.

There are 1,440 minutes in each day. Certainly you can spare fifteen of them to pay attention to yourself if you wish. As any professional musician, athlete, writer, dancer or artist (or anyone else who has developed a special skill) will tell you, you get out of it what you put into it. Paying attention to yourself can be such a perfect use of your time, during which you can learn new skills that will serve you for the rest of your life.

Utensil #3: Writing

The third utensil you'll use to make lemonade out of your lemons is writing. You will do some really great writing because it will be all about *you*. Say anything you want to say when you write. There will be no judgment, critics or required apologies.

If you're feeling embarrassed about the idea of writing down some of the things in your head, *no problem*. If you find yourself critical about what you're writing, join the club. All of this is quite normal. Your inner critic can be transformed while making lemonade, which is another benefit in store for you. *Just write.* Countless times I would begin by writing,

"I don't feel like writing right now. This really sucks ..." And I would continue to write anyway.

Write without hesitation. The more you write, the easier it will become, and the less you will censor or judge yourself. The more you write, the more the chances are that you will become more accepting of your thoughts — which is the point. Actually, do this and someday soon you'll look forward to cozying up to yourself and your writing.

Do you write with pen and paper or type on a computer? What is your writing style? Do you write in long or short sentences? Poetry? Rap? Bullet points? However you do it is 100% the right way for you, and the way that you write, in your most relaxed style, hits the bull's eye.

Remember that this is yours and *only* yours. This is private stuff. Nobody has to know about this but you. Find a safe spot so you can let your thoughts flow.

Offline

Using your three utensils (dreams, going offline and writing), consider your dreams. What are some of them? Take fifteen minutes today and write them down.

On the next page are some examples of how you may want to start your sentences:

I want—

I am going to—

I dream about—

It's going to be amazingly fun to—

I am—

I have—

I will—

Keep going! Add as much to your list as possible.

Is there anything else on your mind? It can be related to this or not. Write it down.

Become free with total abandonment and let yourself dream. Imagine all of the terrific and amazing things that you want to have and feel in your life. When you're finished writing for now, be sure to add the words "These or something better" at the end of your list so that you can allow even more amazing things in that you may not yet have thought about. Be open to the pleasant surprises that are sure to come your way!

This is not a "one shot" list. Go back to it as often as possible when things come up that you would like to invite into your life. The longer your list and the more terrific you feel when you think about it, the better.

CB CB CB

Add the following three ideas to your three utensils of Dreaming, Going Offline and Writing and you will have what you need to conquer your world and make your dreams reality. The ideas are: (1) Neutralization, (2) About Your Thoughts and (3) About Your Emotions.

Idea #1: Neutralization

We will cut open our lemons, however we are going to address them using a special and bladeless knife. The knife is called *neutralization*. Neutralization means to make something neutral, to assign no meaning to it. It is neither good nor bad; it just *is*. It means describing something by providing *just the facts*. Stating what happened. Neutralization is the *bridge* that will connect you to your future self and your future life full of joy and abundance. It will assist you in shifting how you see reality now so that you may then attract the reality you want. Neutralization is the first step in learning to shift how you interpret physical events or things that happen in your life.

When something happens, chances are, without even noticing, you assign meaning to the event, which means that you're on automatic pilot. By practicing neutralization, you start paying attention to your thoughts and are retraining your own thinking process at the same time. And when you do that, you give yourself more opportunities to feel better, to gain new self-understanding, to expand your creativity, and to open up access to the life you want to live.

Here's an example. Let's say that you're outside jogging, and you trip on a broken piece of concrete, lose your balance, and fall down. Chances are that you would automatically think this is a bad thing. To practice neutralization, simply means that you describe what happened without assigning meaning to it. *You make it neutral.*

In this case, what you would do is simply call it what it is. "Wow. I was jogging, tripped and fell down," and THAT'S IT. That is *all* that happened. It does not mean that you are bad or wrong, or that you were not paying attention, or that it is a bad omen. It simply means that you jogged, tripped and fell down.

Let's say that you were jogging, tripped, fell down, and skinned your knee. What happened is: (1) you were jogging, (2) you tripped, (3) you fell down, and (4) you skinned your knee. That is how you slow down your brain to neutral. Then once you are in neutral, you have the ability to assign different meanings to your experiences.

Notice that this example addresses a *non-preferred situation*. The non-preferred situations are the exact ones from which you'll want remove the negativity and judgment. In other words, *you want to neutralize non-preferred situations*. When you experience *preferred situations*, you feel good. And the whole idea is to feel good because when you feel good, your likelihood of *continuing* to attract good situations and experiences increases.

Here is yet another example of neutralizing a non-preferred situation. You have an important meeting at 8:30 tomorrow morning. Before going to bed, you think that you have set your alarm for 7:00 a.m. In the morning, your alarm clock does not ring at 7:00 a.m. and you wake up on your own at 7:45. It turns out that you had set the alarm for 7:00 p.m.

The automatic pilot version goes something like this ... you jump out of bed and you're really upset because you just know that you're going to be late now, and your day (week and month) are completely ruined. You just know it. Plus, on top of that, you may add some form of self-punishment like "I'm stupid and can't do anything right."

Once this train of thought develops ("Train of thought": your first thought is the first car of the train, your next thought is the second car attached to the first car on the train, and so forth ... you have created a *train* of thought), you have pretty much convinced yourself that you're going to have a crappy day. You may even consider just pulling the covers over your head and not getting out of bed because you feel that the day already sucks and it will only get worse.

But since you're paying attention, you then notice your train of thought:

$$- \square - - - - \Rightarrow - - - - - \Rightarrow - - - - \Rightarrow - - - - - \square - -$$

| (I woke up late.) | (I missed my appointment.) | (My day is ruined.) | (I can't do anything right.) | (My life is crap.) |

Become aware of how you automatically jumped ahead several steps in your thinking. *Your final thought will typically have two characteristics: (1) It will be something that you beat yourself up with, and (2) It will reveal a common and habitual belief that you have about yourself that is not true.* In other words, your train of thought will string together several ideas that will ultimately reveal a false belief you have about yourself.

In this particular example, what it translates to in your mind is: "I woke up late. = My life is crap." *Sorry, false belief.* Your life is *not* crap. However, if you believe that your life is crap, it is going to feel like crap as long as you hold that belief in mind. Also, you may feel crappy at the moment, which is just how you feel; let that be okay. There is a difference between feeling crappy at the moment and believing that your life is crap. It's important to learn how to tell the difference.

However, if you *do* believe that your life is crap, chances are that you are going to walk around beaming the message (without even saying a word) that your life is crap, and your world and experiences that day will certainly prove you right because you're unwilling to believe otherwise. You will twist events around to confirm it. ("See, I TOLD you my life is crap!") *Congratulations.* You have guaranteed yourself a bad day.

But what if you neutralized the situation?

As you go to bed at night, you attempt to set your alarm for 7:00 a.m., and in the morning, it does not go off at 7:00 a.m. You wake up on your own at 7:45. You jump out of bed and you're really upset because you know that you're going to be late for your 8:30 appointment. The day is ruined and your life sucks.

This is when you tell yourself to STOP spinning. Put on your Neutralization Hat and observe your thoughts. *Notice that you're spinning out of control in your head.* "Ah, I went from being late to being pissed to thinking that my day is ruined to telling myself that my life sucks. *Interesting.* Okay, I'm going to go back a couple of steps *and just describe what happened.* And what happened? "I tried to set my alarm clock for 7:00 a.m. It didn't ring and I woke up at 7:45." *That is ALL that happened.* Without judgment or criticism, that is all that occurred.

□ – – – – – – – – – – – – – □

(I didn't set the (I woke up later
alarm clock right.) than intended.)

By learning how to deliberately slow down your thinking to simply describing what is going on, you give yourself other possibilities to choose from regarding how you want to see things. You give yourself new choices. So let's say that you slow down your mind to simply describing what occurred. "I thought I had set my alarm clock for 7 a.m. and I woke up at 7:45." And that is all that happened. From there, you might *not* feel compelled to stay in the bed with the covers over your head.

Let's say that you decide to get out of bed and get your day started anyway. You still have 45 minutes; you're not late yet. You can still try to pull things together as quickly as you can, and if you're late, you may not end up being as late as you may have originally thought. You might call to say that you're going to be late, and you could even discover that the person you're meeting is running late as well. You get dressed and head for the train. You get on the train (a later train than expected), and run into an old friend who presents a terrific business opportunity to you. When you're just going with the flow, amazing things can happen. *You never know.*

However you decide to continue your day, by neutralizing your experience of waking up late, you have already relieved some of the stress that in the past would have been automatic. And one less second of stress is a step in the right direction! Change your habitual train of thought (that you usually use to kick your own butt with anyway) by neutralizing the situation, and your stress can lessen and lessen and lessen. When you continue to do this, not only will you feel better ... your health can also improve.

Therefore, noticing your train of thought will help you see where you are in your head about yourself, and you can identify your false beliefs (which you will learn to transform). From there, neutralizing your experiences gives you more options to work with regarding how you decide to view a situation.

Third example: You have a son in third grade who hates doing homework. It has been the same story ever since he started school, and you were hoping that, with the dawn of a new school year, something would have shifted in him and he wouldn't resist doing homework anymore.

But, alas, it is his first night with homework assignments this year, and he is resistant and whining about doing it. You have already "had it!" and your temper, as usual in this situation, gets the best of you. So you're yelling at him about how important it is to do his homework and he's crying. Well, there you go again. It's the same cycle with no solution in sight. And at the same time, you're so tired of yelling at him and feeling like the bad guy.

Now that you understand about neutralization, this would be a situation where you could take some time to observe your train of thought. You'd notice something like this:

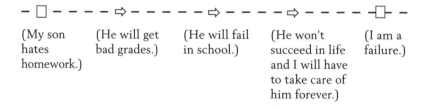

| (My son hates homework.) | (He will get bad grades.) | (He will fail in school.) | (He won't succeed in life and I will have to take care of him forever.) | (I am a failure.) |

You now recognize that as soon as he starts whining about homework, in your mind it looks like this: "My son hates doing homework. = I am a failure." *False belief alert! False belief alert!* No wonder you go immediately to RED and start yelling at him! And continuing to yell at him every night may help create in him exactly what you fear the most: low self-esteem, not living a good life, constant criticism in his head (from *your* voice) and the inability to be independent and thrive.

So slow down your thoughts to really look at this (i.e., "First and foremost, I am *not* a failure." "My son hates doing homework and that is it. Does it mean that he will get bad grades? Maybe, or maybe not." Etc., etc.). You can break it down to acknowledge that you're operating from fear of what may happen as opposed to operating from your positive wishes, which clearly are related to his success. You want him to succeed in school, to be successful in his life, to be happy, and for you to be a good parent.

From neutralization, you may get different perspectives about working with him without losing your temper. By neutralizing the situation, you may discover that you were operating from your personal wish list of qualities for him. When he was a little baby, you may have lovingly watched him sleep and imagined that he was going to be really smart and love school and enjoy learning and doing homework, etc. And now you realize that he doesn't like homework at all, but that does not mean that he isn't smart. It just means that he doesn't like doing homework.

Through neutralization, you notice that this was *your* expectation of him. In reality, it isn't an aspect of who he is — at least not right now. You also notice that you attached your self-value to him doing or not doing his homework (i.e., "If he doesn't like to do homework that means that I am a bad parent").

The fact of the matter is that he still has to do his homework. However, why is it necessary for him to like it? You were hoping that he would enjoy it, but in reality he doesn't. You may make peace with it in your own mind (and realize that you are *not* a failure), and the next time he hems and haws, there will be no "sting" in it for you. You might calmly tell him to cry all he wants, but he will still have to do his homework before he can go play. In time, you may find that he squawks less and gets down to business more quickly, and you can praise and acknowledge him for the fine shift that he is making.

Most importantly, the fact remains that once you slow down your train of thought and observe what meaning you have automatically assigned to any situation, you give yourself an opportunity to *explore other alternatives*. When you practice neutralization, you can simply notice what false beliefs you have about yourself and/or others and you can transform them. When you practice neutralizing situations, you're likely to find that you stress less.

As with any beginning pilot, learning how to navigate after being on automatic pilot takes time, determination and patience. Keep with it even when your mind goes into many different directions at once when you start practicing neutralization. Expect that to happen, which means that it's working! With practice, you'll get the hang of it.

So as you go about your day, notice things around you and practice neutralization. *Just describe things.* A few examples are: "A man just walked through the door," "A girl stuck her tongue out at another girl," and "A woman and a man are walking down the street and laughing." Practice describing what's happening without assigning meaning to it as you think about things, which will give you the opportunity to engage your brain rather than just being on automatic pilot. And if you notice that you're not on automatic pilot and self-criticizing as much, don't judge that either. Just notice it and move on.

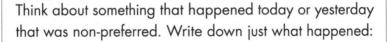

Offline

Think about something that happened today or yesterday that was non-preferred. Write down just what happened:

Here's what happened:

Here's what I originally thought about it:

Here's the false belief I arrived at:

Write down what happened (again):

If I had immediately neutralized the situation, here are a couple of ways I could have seen it differently (use your imagination):

Restate your false belief. (Example: If your false belief is something like "I can't do anything right," the truth is that you do many things right — perhaps just not this time.)

What do you think about the idea of neutralization?

How do you think it can benefit you?

Is there anything else on your mind? It can be related to this or not. Write it down.

Idea #2: About Your Thoughts

Imagine that *you* are like the sky ... a clear blue sky. That is the *"you"* that you know. Now imagine that your thoughts are like *clouds* in the sky. If you know anything about nature, you know that clouds in the sky are never permanent ... they always move, shift and change. Your thoughts are the same way. They are things that you *have*; they are not who you *are*. And they change. *All of the time.* They are always changing, just like the clouds in the sky — big or small, light and bright, gray and menacing, thick like cotton balls, or wispy and thin. They are always moving and changing.

So consider getting comfortable with your thoughts. Be aware of them but don't get distracted by thoughts like "It's bad or wrong for me to feel this way." The fact of the matter is that you DO think and feel the way you do. Just *let it be.* If you give your thoughts and feelings space and don't beat yourself up about them, they will, most assuredly, change and shift more quickly. Let them be okay as they are. And when you find yourself judging them, simply *notice* that you are judging them and move on … *no big deal.* They move just like clouds in the sky.

Offline

Think of a lingering thought you have that you don't feel so great about. Write it down:

What if you did not judge it? What if you just relaxed and let it be? Do you think it may pass more quickly and easily? If yes, why?

If no, why not?

Are you willing to have it change quickly and easily? If yes, why?

If no, are you at least open to the idea?

Is there anything else on your mind? It can be related to this or not. Write it down.

Idea #3: About Your Emotions

From an early age, you were trained to understand how your physical body works. Perhaps you were taught to stay away from a hot stove, to not play with sharp objects, and/or to not run in the middle of the street. Your emotional body is as important as your physical body; yet if you are like many of us, you may have been taught to fear or ignore it.

The last thing you may want to do is feel stuff because sometimes feeling hurts. The only problem with suppressing emotion when you're hurting is that your ability to feel joy, excitement and happiness gets locked up as well.

Consider this ... What if you perceived your emotions as "Energy-in-motion," in other words *E-motion?* When something impacts you, it is simply energy. It's simply something that impacts you. When you allow that energy to have motion (when you *express it*), you allow the impactful experience, whether big or small, to flow through you rather than get stuck and wreak havoc on your body.

Emotions (or, energy-in-motion) act like ocean waves. A *wave* starts small then begins to build until it crashes to the shore, then it retreats. Waves are never permanent and have a *predictable* cycle. Your emotions, *when expressed*, are the same way. They reach a peak and then they retreat. It is a *very* predictable pattern.

For example, when you feel happy, you're more inclined to ride that wave as long as possible — which is terrific. However, when you feel a wave of sadness or hurt or anger coming on, and you ride *that* out (with harm to none, *including yourself*), *it will eventually subside, then go away!* You ride it out by letting it *safely* express itself. We will talk more about this when we add water to our lemons, but for now, consider this initial concept when it comes to your emotions. Their journey is predictable (which hopefully gives you a sense of empowerment, safety and comfort while you look at the idea of releasing emotion).

It is worth repeating that your thoughts *and* emotions are things that you *have*. They are NOT who you *are*. Consider that you are multidimensional. You are much bigger and way more special than just being a bundle of thoughts and emotions! So let them be. They have every right to exist, and you are bigger than they are. You can either allow them to express or not. You are the boss and are in the driver's seat.

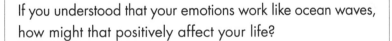

Offline

If you understood that your emotions work like ocean waves, how might that positively affect your life?

Is there anything else on your mind? It can be related to this or not. Write it down.

愈 愈 愈

Pep Talk #1

To summarize, you have three utensils (Dreams, Going Offline, and Writing) and three ideas (Neutralization,

Clouds and Waves) to use as you begin to make lemonade. Be willing to remember that your experiences, thoughts and emotions are things that you *have*. They are not what you *are*. You are much more than that! Once you begin dreaming, writing and neutralizing situations, you become lighter, and you'll automatically start the process that will help you attract more of what you truly want.

These are tools that you can use for the rest of your life. They alone can help you to transform your experiences and live a happier and more contented life.

It's time, here and now, to transform your world. How good do you want your life to be? How amazing can you make it? How much love can you invite into your life? You create it from the inside out and it is *up to you*!

It's really an amazing existence when we learn how to navigate life from the inside out rather than the outside in (the latter is what we typically do). Here's an analogy. You have to run some errands. You get in the car, and start it up. In order to steer the car, you put your hands on the rear-view mirror instead of on the steering wheel. You can go straight for a while, maybe, but then you start bumping into stuff and hitting walls. Meanwhile, you cannot figure out why you can't get to where you want to go! So you hit a wall, put the car in reverse, put your hands on the rear-view mirror, back up, and go again. And it is inevitable that you will veer off course again because you're not using the proper instrument for guiding the car. So you stay stuck, trying to navigate a car with the rear-view mirror. It can become crazy-making (like Albert Einstein said, insanity is doing the same thing over and over again and expecting a different result).

So after looking for outside remedies for your happiness for years and years (i.e., driving with your hands on the rear-view mirror), at some point, *if you are lucky*, you become disillusioned with it. You might break down, feeling like there is nowhere else to turn. All I can say is "thank goodness." Because with breakdowns come breakthroughs. During a breakdown, you are open to suggestions. You can learn to take your hands off the rear-view mirror and put them firmly on the steering wheel. From there, you can navigate your life more easily, and find that you are indeed finally moving in the direction you would like to go.

When you do, you begin to realize how truly amazing you are, and how remarkable your life truly is. It's a very personal journey that can be quite magical and fun.

Time to make lemonade. Lemons, water and sugar is all it takes. *Let's do it!*

Lemons

*"Out of suffering have emerged the strongest souls;
the most massive characters are seared with scars."*

—Khalil Gibran

Definition

What are *lemons*? Simply put, "lemons" are beliefs and/or experiences that have compromised your physical, emotional and/or spiritual well-being.

Once again:

Lemons are beliefs and/or experiences that have compromised your physical, emotional and/or spiritual well-being.

Using neutralization, here is a sample list of lemons (in no particular order):

- My beloved pet ran away or died.
- I continue to feel disrespect because of my skin color.

- I lost my job.
- I was teased a lot as a child.
- I was taught to be suspicious of anyone who doesn't look like me.
- I felt disrespected because of my religious beliefs (gender or nationality).
- I was physically (emotionally and/or sexually) abused.
- There were complications during my birth and I have ongoing physical (and/or mental) challenges.
- I did not grow up with my mother (or father).
- My mother (and/or father) was domineering, controlling and/or smothering.
- My marriage did not work out.
- I felt unprotected as a child.
- I was born in a war-torn country and saw people get killed.
- My father (and/or mother) was addicted to drugs (alcohol, food and/or anger).
- My parents had a nasty divorce.
- My parents stayed together but argued and fought a lot.
- I was taught (and agree) that people of other religions are wrong.
- I had to take care of my brothers and sisters when I was still a child myself.
- I was misunderstood a lot.
- I felt empty a lot.

This list is only a *sample* of the types of lemons that you might have experienced. It is heartbreaking that there are so many things, big and small, that may have compromised your well-being. Certainly no list can cover all of them.

None of us are exempt from pain. The human experience is wrought with land mines. We encounter experiences and people that can test our very sanity. However, if you express yourself well, hurt when you are in pain (knowing that it will fade away), and are living a life full of joy with constant unexpected pleasures, you won't have any lemons because you already know how to handle your life's experiences.

But if your quality of life is not what you would like for it to be, that means that there is at least one belief or experience in your life that qualifies as a lemon. It is holding you back from getting to know your true self because you spend your time constantly trying to respond to it (or avoid it). It is time to resolve this.

Don't force yourself to come up with a lemon. You do not have to try to recall unpleasant memories that you aren't already aware of.

NOW is all that matters. If you remember unpleasant memories now, they are impacting you NOW.

Time is an *illusion*. Certainly we think in linear terms (i.e., one thing happens then another thing happens, 1999 rolls into 2000, then 2001, etc.); however when it comes to your *inner* world, there is no time. In fact, an experience that you remember from your past *becomes present* when you think of it. And however you *feel* when you think about it impacts you *right now.*

For example, you listen to a song that you loved when you were eight years old. When you hear that song today, it will "bring you back" in time to when you were eight. You remember the smells, the room, and your frame of mind at that time. All of the things surrounding it can become clear as day, even if just for a split second.

Using this idea, here is an example of a prior event's current impact. Let's say that when you were younger you were riding your bike and your neighbor's pesky little terrier chased you home, and you felt really scared. Now you have children yourself and your three-year-old is smiling and reaching out his little hand to pet a cute little friendly terrier. If *you* feel fear or concern or want the baby to stop for whatever reason, it may be because that event from your past has been triggered *now.* A lemon is at work, otherwise you would be able to take the situation at face value — seeing that your toddler (*and* the little terrier) is curious and friendly, end of story.

If you take a look and find that there are some less than good feelings there, now, Now, NOW is the time for you to fill those painful holes with love, encouragement and support. We will do this together. I will coach you at transforming your lemons.

Take a quick scan. If you can identify at least one lemon in your past (or one that occurred last week or even today), please acknowledge yourself right now for still functioning on the planet in whatever capacity you find yourself. *I'm not kidding.* With deep respect, I applaud you. Commend yourself for continuing to survive, despite your lemons. It's a testament to your strength, fortitude and resilience!

Let this idea simmer for a while. Be willing to look at yourself from the point of view of being a survivor. The definition of *survivor,* according to the Random House dictionary, is: *"A person who continues to function or prosper in spite of opposition, hardship or setbacks."* And that would be YOU!

In your offline time, look in the mirror and acknowledge the survivor that you are. Congratulate yourself on surviving! Do this more than once or twice. Congratulate yourself every time you pass a mirror (even if you're embarrassed by the practice). And if in your survivor status you feel like you're functioning yet are really longing to prosper at a higher level, let's turn that corner now.

CB CB CB

Lemons–A Closer Look

Simply put, here is what you (and what we all) need, and perhaps yearn for:

- You need to be acknowledged.
- You need to be understood.
- You need to feel safe.
- You need to feel valued.
- You need to be loved.

When you carry a lemon with you right now, it means that you didn't get what you needed at that time to get over what happened. For whatever reason, you didn't have the opportunity to express your feelings at the time you were originally hurt and your need to be acknowledged, understood and loved went unmet.

The fact of the matter is that, at the time, you needed more encouragement and support. Or, perhaps, you could have used a different kind of encouragement and support. If you had received the right kind and right amount of encouragement and support at the time, your lemon would already be lemonade!

You may be like so many of us who, as we become adults, look to others not to share love, but to fulfill our unmet needs. Have you yearned for the one person who will hold you and tell you that everything is going to be okay? Do you think that you'll be fixed if you marry someone with money? Have you found yourself disappointed over and over again after thinking that you have found the love of your life, best friend, job or home?

If you continuously try to acquire things or be with certain people that you think can help you feel better about yourself and your life, it won't accomplish what you think it will. What you are doing, really, is continuing to operate in response to your lemons and unmet needs. By definition, acquiring "outside" stuff cannot satisfy your feeling of lack on the inside.

Here's the real kicker … *We are all in the same boat!* We all have lemons in some way, and we are all walking wounded to some degree. We constantly seek to fulfill our unmet needs with other people, places and things. We're not looking to (or in a position to) *give* love, we are looking to *receive* love. So we're constantly looking around to see what we can be, do, feel or have in order for us to feel better about ourselves and our lives. When the majority of us are *seeking* love, fewer are in the position to give it, and we remain unfulfilled.

The exercise is *not* about blaming your parents, guardians or others for your lemons. Your parents and guardians did the best they thought they could. Blaming others won't free you.

The exercise is *not* about seeking love, encouragement and support from others first because that will not fulfill you in the way you need to be fulfilled.

The exercise *now* is about taking responsibility for your own quality of life, and responding to your own unmet needs.

Responsibility simply means having the ability to respond.
Response-ability = responsibility.

You have the ability to respond to the experiences in
your life, and you are free to begin to make a shift whenever
you're ready. Nobody else *but you* has the best ability to
respond to the state of your well-being now. If you have
ever taken a flight on an airplane, certainly you are familiar
with the instructions that are provided before takeoff — in
case of a drop in cabin pressure, put on your *own* oxygen
mask first and then assist others.

Think about it. *No one knows exactly what you need more
than you do.* What could someone say to you that would
completely melt your heart and make your day? You may
have dreamed about it a thousand times. Well, why wait
to find that perfect someone to see if they can peer into
your heart and soul, then give you what you need? Cut to
the chase and learn to give it to yourself *right now.*

You can acknowledge, process, then heal your lemons.
You can grow, very safely, and develop a true sense of
honor for yourself. You will acknowledge your strengths
and your value. From there, you will learn how to give
yourself the love and respect that you yearn for. And
when you do, you will attract it from others as well. You
will no longer rely on it from others first because you'll
already be able to feel it from within first, and it will be
very, very sweet. You will be self-reliant, fulfill your own

needs, and blaze forth with your unique gifts and talents to live the life of your dreams.

You have the innate ability to heal yourself. Working with your lemons marks the beginning of your new life, full of transformation and previously unimaginable fun. When you *reconnect* with yourself, you can discover your own true voice. You'll uncover who you *really* are, underneath all the stuff that may have limited your beliefs about what you can be, do and have. You'll have your hands firmly on the steering wheel. You will experience, firsthand, the greatest comeback story in the history of the world!

This is YOUR life. How do YOU want to live YOUR life? How would you like your story to be when you look back on your life? Would you like to say at the end of the day that you *went* for it despite your challenges? Would you like for your story to be that you triumphed over adversity? Would you like to be able to say that you did your best with what you knew at any given time? Any way your life story will read is fine. It's up to *you*. You are in the driver's seat and can make of your life whatever you want.

CB CB CB

Lemons — Your Blueprint for Success

The perfect starting point for making lemonade from lemons is where you are *right now*. Your lemons are the blueprint for your amazing new life.

Here are some examples of the blueprint from your lemons and the result of their transformation:

Here's what you got. (Lemons)	Here's what you wanted.	Here's what you'll learn to say and give to yourself. (Lemonade)
My mother didn't love me.	My mother's love	LOVE ("I am your mother now. You are amazing and I love you beyond measure. I will always tell you how much I love and honor you.")
My father wasn't in my life.	My father to be in my life	BELONGING ("I am your father now. I've always been with you and always cheered for you. I'm so proud of you and will be forever.")
I lost my job.	I want to earn a living to support myself (and my family).	SUPPORT ("You have what you need to ensure the well-being of your family. No matter what, we will survive and from there, we will thrive.")
My marriage failed.	A successful marriage	INTIMACY ("You have the ability to have an intimate and successful relationship with another person.")

When it comes to ideas such as joy, transformation and love, we have a tendency to understand them intellectually but never move beyond that understanding. It's time to have courage and go deeper, so that you can move from the intellectual, conceptual understanding (the "I shoulds") to the true experience ("I am"). When you take responsibility for your life ... when you respond to your lemons ... miracles can happen.

> *"The deeper sorrow carves into your being*
> *the more joy you can contain."*
>
> —Khalil Gibran

Offline

Think about just one of your lemons using neutralization (simply describe what happened). What do you think might be the lemonade that you will enjoy?

This is what happened:

This is what I wanted:

This is what I can enjoy because of it:

Is there anything else on your mind? It can be related to this or not. Write it down.

Water

"We think sometimes that poverty
is only being hungry, naked and homeless. The
poverty of being unwanted, unloved and uncared
for is the greatest poverty. We must start in our own
homes to remedy this kind of poverty."

—Mother Teresa

How do you get from lemons to lemonade? You cut open the lemons and then add water. Here's where you start crossing the bridge from where you are to your future self, full of energy, empowerment, a true sense of deservability and joy.

You have spread your wings to dare to dream about what you want to attract into your life. *Keep dreaming.* Make your dreams bigger and sweeter! Close your eyes, breathe deeply and fill yourself up with good feelings in anticipation of what is to come.

Perhaps you are also starting to go offline and do some writing, and you've mulled over the ideas about neutralization, your thoughts and your emotions. Wherever you are with your process, whether you are going offline or not, writing or not, *trust that you are exactly where you need to be.* There are no "shoulds" or "have to's." This is your life and your experience. You have the freedom to do whatever you want to do or *don't* want to do with it.

If, however, you're feeling a "should" with respect to this (e.g., "I *should* be doing some writing now," or "I *should* go offline at some point today"), substitute the words "want to" anytime you have a "should." Therefore, the thought becomes "I *want to* do some writing now," or "I *want to* go offline at some point today." Notice the difference once you substitute "want to" for "should."

(As a side note, do you think that you must push yourself with the "should do's"? Just be aware of it. You may feel like you wouldn't do anything if the critical voice inside of you — the taskmaster — isn't pushing you. When you start with "Oh, I *should* do this," or "I *should* do that," it basically means that you don't *want* to do whatever it is but are being forced to. On the other hand, when you practice saying, "I *want* to do this," it moves you from feeling forced to actively choosing a course of action. It puts you in the driver's seat and empowers you to move forward from an act of will rather than from an act of coercion. It moves you from an energy of enslavement [in your own mind] to an energy of freedom and creativity [in your own mind]. When you proceed through an act of will rather than from feeling forced to, you can go farther and faster and are *more* productive and creative. Therefore, notice your thinking habits in this way and substitute "want to" for "should" whenever you think about it and observe the difference in how you feel.)

C8 C8 C8

Listening

Now it is time to become the world's best listener — *to yourself.* There is nobody in the entire world more important to listen to first than yourself. Listening is step one when adding water to your lemons.

Has the fear or grumbling started yet? Hopefully so, because it won't be there one day and you'll marvel at how far you've come!

Oftentimes we avoid listening to ourselves at all cost. We immerse ourselves with distractions, such as shopping, our work, our children, food, alcohol, sex — all to avoid listening to the ongoing dialogue in our head.

You have many voices within you. You may feel like avoiding that fact; but if you tell yourself the truth, you know they are there. *Identify them. Listen to them. Get to know them.*

By listening to them, you will be able to understand how you arrived at some false beliefs that you may have about yourself. Those may be contained in the menacing voices inside of you that you run away from.

For example, let's say that your parents divorced when you were still a child. You may have developed a habitual false belief about yourself in order to make sense out of the experience, and acted out as a result of it. And if you did, *this* is the lemon to transform so that you can live your best life. You will be able to determine what it is by starting to listen to yourself, and then put the pieces together about how you responded to what happened.

Let's say that when your father moved out, you lost interest in school, or started being a bully. Whatever you *did* was a reaction to how you *felt* about his departure. If you look at it, going back to neutralization, your train of thought might have been something like this:

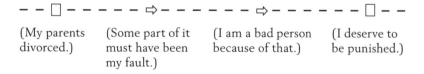

| (My parents divorced.) | (Some part of it must have been my fault.) | (I am a bad person because of that.) | (I deserve to be punished.) |

Notice the false beliefs starting quickly. Your parents' divorce was *not* your fault. Your parents' divorce does *not* make you a bad person, and you most definitely did not (and do not) deserve to keep punishing yourself in whatever ways you do it.

The whisper inside of you that keeps saying, "You deserve to be punished and are no good" can be considered menacing and you may constantly try to run from it, yet you keep attracting punishing situations. *No amount of positive thinking will overtake that which you truly believe (or fear).* The fact of the matter is that you may still be angry he left, and when you peel back your anger, underneath it is hurt and sadness. And once you allow yourself to *feel* the hurt and sadness, then healing happens (the how-to is coming up!).

As of now, the jig is up for the menacing voice. Why? Because, paradoxically, when you give it airtime by simply acknowledging it without fearing or judging this voice, it loses its power. You say to it, "So you think I deserve to be punished, huh? Well, that is simply not true. They were grown people and I was the child who needed protection and love." The menacing voice might even get louder and argue with you about your non-deservability, but only for a while. It cannot outlast you. *It* relies on *you* for its survival.

Acknowledging and embracing the aspect of yourself that you consider menacing or foreboding allows you to transform how you view it. Make no mistake about it. When you suppress the menacing voice, and when you fear it, the *VOICE* will control *YOU.* When you acknowledge then learn to express your menacing voice safely (thus transforming it), you realize that you are bigger and stronger than *it* is and you invoke a sense of empowerment that might feel unimaginable right now. Once you transform it, you will find that the voice is the holder of your passion and inner fire — the very attributes that you will need to create what you want in your life!

However you feel about your menacing voice — whether it is just annoying, petrifying or debilitating — consciously neutralize it. No more attaching the meaning that it is bad. Be willing to simply acknowledge it and continue on with your life. Allow it to release and express itself safely (*the how-to is coming up!*). As time goes by, it will transform while other voices within you (such as the nurturing and praising voices and those that want to dance and sing and smile at everybody!) gain strength.

You will come to understand that *you* are bigger than your inner villain. *Give it light.* Take the wind out of its sails by talking about it and letting it express itself in your writing. Chances are it actually seeks closure on an unaddressed lemon or two. When it is critical, ask it what is its positive wish for you. What, deep down, does it want to you enjoy, or be, do and/or have? Know that *you* know there is a positive wish in it for you, even if your inner villain doesn't know it yet.

Expect it to *try* to get louder and rebel against you. Hold your ground (simply by staying alive and doing the writing with harm to none) and you'll find it getting smaller. It can eventually say, "Well, I have been waiting for her to get the courage to let me express myself. She's actually befriending me. Now I can transform; I can now share my positive wishes with her. She's stepped up and can receive the gifts that I have been protecting!"

And, in time, you may find that the joke is on you. Once you have the courage to face the demons living inside of you and let them express themselves safely, you'll find that the big, angry, menacing voice is an illusion — that it is actually a scared and vulnerable cute little creature that needs *your* love and attention.

In the practice of listening, you'll learn to break things down. You will come to understand that you had operated under many false beliefs. Your lemons are *not* your fault in any way. You will now know that in your heart. You aren't a bad person. You will also now know this in your heart. You are strong and courageous for just breathing. You will now know that in your heart too.

Keep in mind that you are not the only one who has those thoughts among all the other kinds of thoughts. If we were being honest, and there was a "Menacing Thoughts Live Here Too" T-shirt, we would all be wearing one. We *all* have different aspects to ourselves. Here are some examples: the hopeful part, the crazy part, the angry part, the sad part, the Perfectionist, the Nurturer, the Wise One, the Magical Child, the Slacker, the Teenager, the Jokester, the Passionate One, the Critical Parent … you name it! Because of this, we have all kinds of thoughts and perspectives milling about. Constant internal chatter is not unusual at all!

As a result (especially in the case of our inner villains), there are aspects of us that we don't want, don't want to care for, and most certainly can't imagine loving. Therefore, there are parts of you that are unwanted, unloved and uncared for. When you want, love and care for even the menacing aspects of yourself, you'll find your true home within you. You'll find that you can slow down your mind at will because you accept and allow all of your different facets to exist.

What if you operated under the assumption that everything you think and feel is okay? No matter what it is and no matter what anyone else may have told you, what if you adopted a belief that it is all valid — that how you feel is valid and there are perfectly good reasons for thinking and believing the way you do (even when you don't know what they are)?

Start getting used to the idea that how you think is simply how you think. It simply is what it is. There is nothing bad or wrong about it. It simply *exists*; it *just is*. Be willing to neutralize your thoughts, feelings and beliefs. *Everything* you think is valid, or else you wouldn't be thinking it. It would not exist.

Imagine that they each float around on their own little clouds. They float in and out, come and go. They are a part of your inner landscape. They are part of what makes you uniquely who you are, and you're truly one of a kind.

The only time your thoughts and feelings are harmful is when you act out against yourself or others. At no time is it acceptable to injure yourself or others. You may *want* to. You may *think* about it, and if that helps you process your anger, it's fine. Just don't act on it physically!

As a matter of fact, let us start a "Harm to None" Club right now, and the rules are as follows:

1. I am a member of *Lemons, Lemonade & Life*'s Harm to None Club.
2. I hereby proclaim that all that I think and feel is okay, and I am okay to explore my inner workings without fear or judgment.
3. I am willing to accept how I think and believe (*however* that may be), and I am willing to allow others to do the same for themselves.
4. I will, here and now, move forward in my life with harm to none. If I have been acting out against myself and/or others in any way, I will now *stop* that behavior and focus on my self-healing.

When you give yourself permission to *think* how you think and *feel* how you feel *without judgment or apology*, you will naturally transform your life. Be willing to think of your thoughts, all of them, as 100% acceptable, and with harm to none, including yourself. Once you do, you can come to understand that your thoughts and beliefs are your friends and your protectors. You may also find that they are your own personal and greatest entertainers! Once you have the courage to safely express them, you gain your strength and your gifts, and you will be amazed at how humorous and fun it can be to just listen to the goings on in your head.

To improve the world, we have to start somewhere. *Why not start with ourselves?* Imagine the crime rate decreasing as the Harm to None Club membership increases!

In other words, take care of yourself. *LISTEN.*

> *"To forget how to dig the earth and to tend the soil is to forget ourselves."*

—Mohandas Karamchand Gandhi

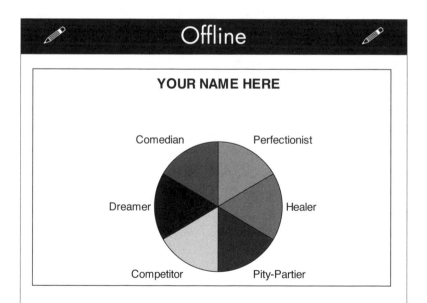

Don't fear your voices. They are part of you. Give a name to the different voices in your head. Just describe them. Call them who they are. Here are more examples: the Inner

Critic, the Saint, the Child, the Complainer, the Adolescent, the Victim, the Protector, and so on. Put them in your pie chart, and continue to add more slices to the pie chart as you identify more voices inside yourself.

If they are screaming, just breathe and listen. Notice them. Identify them. Ask for their positive wishes. You are bigger than they are. They are a part of you. They are like clouds in the sky and they will transform.

With the ones that you find particularly annoying or worrisome, what would you imagine are hidden within them that you can use to your benefit?

What else is on your mind right now? It can be related to this or not. Write it down.

Practice listening and write about what is on your mind, <u>without judgment,</u> for at least 15 minutes today. Just call it what it is, whatever IT is, however you want to say it. And when you say it, identify which part of you is speaking. Allow it to speak and acknowledge it without judgment.

CB CB CB

Releasing Emotion

While it's necessary and important to learn to protect our physical bodies by following rules and obeying laws in order to stay alive and get along with others (e.g., don't touch a hot stove, or walk into traffic), many of us have been taught to suppress or ignore our *emotional* bodies. We are conditioned to think that it is bad to cry or dangerous to feel. We learn how to be cool to protect ourselves. To not get too excited about anything so that we're not disappointed when things don't turn out as planned. To not be supported when we feel certain ways or feel anything at all!

We're actually afraid of emotion. We're taught to ignore it, or be ashamed about it. "Boys don't cry" is like a death sentence because our beautiful boys are not able to learn how to process what they feel … it just gets jumbled up inside and their ability to recognize and express how they feel can be stunted. When we get into the habit of withholding expression of our sadness and/or anger, it builds up inside of us.

When we were hurt as children, healing would have naturally occurred if we were able to express ourselves, and then were acknowledged and understood. When expression, acknowledgement and understanding happen, our wounds heal naturally then disappear and we move on with life. However, when something hurt our feelings and we cried about it, many times we may have been ridiculed, chastised or punished just for crying. Thus we learn to suppress our emotions in order to survive.

Or we may have continued to express ourselves and did not receive the acknowledgement and understanding we sought. In both scenarios, our love, hope and innocence go into hiding. Those parts of us never die, but depending upon the severity of our suppressed or unfulfilled emotion, they can get buried.

And as this continues to be buried, our unmet needs begin to accumulate and we put on whatever brave face may be required, and we act in ways that will ensure our survival. We may not have received the love we so desperately needed but we did (and continue to do) what we had to do to survive. We may not have received the amount of guidance we needed to successfully navigate in the world but we did (and continue to do) what we have to do to survive. When we did something well, we may not have gotten the support, acknowledgement and encouragement that we needed to develop a strong, positive sense of self. When we had questions, they may have gone unanswered, or perhaps we were punished for having asked them. Maybe nobody listened to us when we had something to say.

Results of Suppressing Emotion:

- Physical illness
- Lack of connection/intimacy with others
- Inability to feel joy and/or happiness
- Growth of inner distress

Everyone has their own threshold for pain. One person may be able to tolerate regular beatings, whereas someone else may be devastated by being hit just once. *This isn't about someone else's experiences; this is about your own. You feel how you feel and you were impacted however you were impacted. There is no comparison between your pain and anyone else's.*

Minimizing the impact of challenging experiences is a commonly used tool for survival, and appropriately so. Yet we often then continue the habit of minimizing our pain throughout our life. When anything comes up that evokes even the thought of feeling something, we run from it when in fact, running *towards* it and getting *through* it holds the key to our best problem-solving capabilities, true clarity and joy.

Now that you are older, you can work with that old habit. Now you can learn to acknowledge and honor your experiences and move forward with a deeper feeling of confidence and support. This will help you live joyously much more quickly.

In the midst of trying to suppress emotion, the desire to express emotion is ever present. Here is an example. You're at an amusement park and you're on a roller-coaster. It climbs to the top and you know that, very shortly, it will drop. And when it drops, what typically happens? You scream! They may be screams of terror or horror, or screams mixed with laughter, who knows? But it is energy-in-motion being allowed to express itself.

Here is another example. You're in a movie theater watching a comedy. When something is funny, you laugh (the movie-makers sure hope so). You're impacted by something that happens on the screen and you allow yourself the ability to respond to it in the form of laughter. Or if you are watching a scary movie and something jumps out unexpectedly, you may gasp or scream. That is energy-in-motion.

Lots of us enjoy watching sad movies, love stories, thrillers and comedies because it gives us an excuse to explore our emotions in a dark and quiet place. It gives us the opportunity to allow energy to have motion.

You may operate under the assumption that if you ignore the pain it won't affect you. People often say, "Just get over it and move on." However, when you try to feel a certain way, talk yourself out of believing what you feel deep down, or minimize the impact of a lemon in your life, you automatically create more of a gap between you and your true self. You rob yourself of the ability to reconnect with who you really are, which is *underneath* the emotion, underneath the pain. From your true self is where all your dreams can materialize and transforming the lemon is how you get there.

The idea of "get over it" is a really good one, actually. Think about it in this way: when you get *over* something (when you get over "it"), this means that you are *bigger* than "it." When you avoid something, you fear looking at it because it feels too big, or too heavy or too deep and painful to approach. That is when you believe deep down, that *it* is bigger than *you* are.

The fact of the matter is that you are bigger than your experiences. When you "get over it," you begin to understand your own strength and power and you have the ability to handle anything in your life. When you "get over it," it looks something like this:

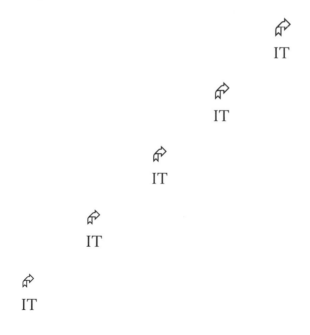

Every time you get *over* something, you become bigger than IT is. You get lighter, stronger and more empowered. Things that would have remained with you and weighed heavily on you can just roll off without even impacting you. You clear up space inside of you and attract more of what you want!

You get over something by neutralizing it, calling this what it is *for you*, releasing whatever emotion is associated with it without judgment, then allowing it to heal naturally.

If the thought of honoring unpleasant experiences and qualities makes you squirm, that is quite all right. Just understand that you are afraid of the parts of you that feel dark. Your life's shocking experiences that you have been down on yourself about seek light. They seek acknowledgment and understanding. It is a paradox. When light, in any small way, hits the darkness, it is transformed. It is only your *fear, judgment and blocked emotions about* them that give them the illusion of being bigger than you.

Long-Term Results of Releasing Emotion:

- Improved health
- The ability to connect with yourself (and then with others)
- The ability to experience true joy and/or happiness
- Dissolving of inner darkness and increase of lightness
- Mental and emotional clarity

Offline

Think about your lemons. How do you cover up your hurt? How have you responded to pain and disappointment in your life? Do you just keep busy or drown yourself in your work? Do you live with constant feelings of anger? Do you use humor? Withdraw? Are you aggressive? Ask yourself these questions with the intent of getting to really understand yourself by familiarizing yourself with how you work.

Explore without judgment the beliefs you have about expressing emotion. Do you think it is bad or wrong or unsafe? Do you fear letting it out? Why?

After writing about why you might be afraid of expressing most or some of your emotion, identify which aspect of you is talking. Is it your Child? Or perhaps it is your Inner Critic? Welcome it with acknowledgement and understanding because, given your background and beliefs, it makes perfect sense to feel that way.

Now call upon your inner Nurturer, Wise One or Healer. What does it have to say about expressing emotion? Allow it to speak to and comfort the other aspect of yourself that is fearful. Write until you feel a sense of calm, reassurance and/or hope.

Is there anything else on your mind?

രു രു രു

Time to Add Water

Here is where you use the tools and understanding to respond to your lemons. When you take action, the magic starts. The *combination of listening and honoring your thoughts and safely releasing emotion* equals adding water to your lemons. This process of adding water will profoundly shift your life. The more water you add, the less tart the lemons become.

Working with water is a completely OFFLINE process. Learn to become comfortable with expressing emotion with yourself. You may think that expressing your anger, rage, sorrow, etc. with others will get you the understanding you seek; however you may not receive what you need. But when you express alone, you can *always* give yourself exactly what you need. While expressing offline, you will say all of the things you want to say to someone, and in return you will hear all of the things you would want someone to say to you. You will learn to say *all of it first* and it will change your life.

The whole idea is to give your feelings a voice, a way to express, in a safe place. Once your feelings are able to release, they will feel much better, having been allowed the opportunity to express themselves. From there, you can gain more clarity. Allow them to be soothed and they will transform.

Here are three ways to release: (1) via your physical body, (2) in writing, and (3) through visualization. Each of them is very effective, and it depends on your style and what you find works best for you as to how you will use them.

They are interchangeable. You may find that writing works best at one point, then when you release next time you may get physical or go right into visualization.

You may also find that you use all three of them as you ride an emotional wave. You might start physically by banging on pillows, then feel the need to write. Writing may transition into banging on pillows again. When you calm down, visualization might do the trick, and you could feel calm and peaceful again (or maybe for the first time ever!).

Let's put this into action by cutting open a lemon and adding water to it. The following is an example.

Let's say that you just went through a grueling, two-week interview process for a job that you really needed and wanted, and you find out that you didn't get it. Make no mistake about it; this is a lemon — *an experience that compromised your physical and/or emotional well-being.* You are very angry and extremely disappointed.

When you're alone and in a safe place, let it out. Express your anger and disappointment. If getting physical feels right, cry. Beat on pillows. Scream. Jump up and down. Lean over and breathe out really hard. Let your body do whatever it needs to do to ride the wave of the emotion you're experiencing.

While you're riding the wave by kicking and screaming or crying, etc., your disappointment may say something like "I can't BELIEVE I didn't get the job." (Or you may be expressing this by writing it out.) Whether you are saying it while being physical or by writing, your response will be:

"Yes, I hear you." Your anger may say, "That jerk! I want to rip his face off for not hiring me." Your response will be: "Yes, I understand … I get it." Your hurt may say, "How could that have happened when I was perfect for it???" and you say, "I know, right? I understand totally. Yep, you are SO right." Your Inner Critic might say, "See, I told you so." And your Inner Defender might say, "Give her a break, she worked hard for it."

While you're expressing *exactly* how you feel without censor or judgment, say "Yes" to everything you are feeling. Honor your feelings … let them be okay, exactly as is. Your deepest wish is to be acknowledged and understood, and it is imperative to acknowledge and understand yourself first. Understand that by doing this *you fulfill your own needs* that may have previously gone unmet.

Continue to ride the waves. *Let it all out.* As you're letting it out, other insights can come into play. The next layer, after you release your initial anger and disappointment, might be your Consoling Self. "They didn't deserve you anyway," and/or "I really wanted it but was always concerned about the hours." Next, your Determined Self might say something like "Screw those people. I'll find something better and with the hours I prefer." *Acknowledge all of it.*

You have a Nurturing and Wise Self that you were born with that is ready to serve you. Your Nurturing and Wise Self knows *exactly* what you need to hear to get over the disappointment, something which will enable you to move forward with your job search with a fresh perspective. The disappointment of not getting the other job will slowly fade away, all because you rode the wave!

Your Nurturing and Wise Self won't be able to reach you with its clarity, faith and optimism when your anger and disappointment are muffling it. When you acknowledge and validate your anger and disappointment, in time they will subside and wisdom can creep in. This is a natural occurrence!

After you ride the waves, you may feel tired, worn out and/or sleepy — which is common. Energetic release shifts your body and afterwards it will integrate what just happened. If you can lie down for a while, do it. If you can't, relax and take some deep breaths, then continue with your day but be gentle with yourself. If another wave of sadness comes up, go somewhere and respond to it by letting it express itself and call upon your Consoling Self to be present as well.

Offline

Think about one of your lemons. Pick one, any one. It could be from three minutes ago or forty years ago. Whatever size the lemon, it is perfect to use.

Describe what happened:

How did you feel about it? (Really allow yourself to express this as fully as you can!)

What could someone else have said or done that would have helped you get over it?

Give yourself that acknowledgement, encouragement and understanding right now. Keep going until you feel better.

Is there anything else on your mind? Talk about it now.

Keep reminding yourself that releasing your emotions has a predictable cycle. You may be in agony at the moment but it will pass when you respond to it. When you feel a wave of sadness or hurt or anger coming on, ride it out and it will eventually subside.

You can take control of your life by applying these tools in any situation. With time and practice, you will come to understand that there isn't anything you cannot handle because you know *how* to do it. Find a way to be alone and let it safely express itself. Remember that *it* is a part of *you* and you are big enough to let it release.

If you can't find a way to be alone at the moment you identify a wave of emotion coming on, be willing to muster up some self-control and hold on until you are alone and can safely release. This is more for your benefit than anyone else's. You have every right to feel how you are feeling. Do not express it in ways where you may make a bad situation worse or have to apologize later for some scary behavior now. Again, when you are alone, you have the right to do what you need to do to release without censorship or judgment. But in the presence of others, your ability to safely express becomes diluted.

✎ Offline ✎

When you're in crisis, here is your script (keep in mind that sometimes you just need to cry, kick and scream and vent in general for quite a while before you can even *think* about thinking):

Describe what happened:

What does your critic want to say?

How does your Crazy Person feel about it? Let it out.

What does your anger have to say? Let it out.

What does your Child have to say? Let it out.

Let all of them have their say and express it.

As the wave starts to subside, call on your Consoler and Nurturer. What do they have to say? Let them talk for as long as they need to. Listen and/or write it down.

What would you have preferred to have at that time? What are your positive wishes?

> Give yourself those words of encouragement and support right now.
>
> Keep breathing.

Here is the real kicker … When you set the intention to live the life of your dreams, *situations will automatically arise that challenge you to express your emotions.* Learn to expect them! When you allow energy to have motion in current non-preferred situations, it can help you express old, unresolved hurts that are still within you when they arise. And when you start healing the old, unresolved hurts with the same method, your inner world clears up, and you reap the benefits by learning that you can handle anything that comes your way. This will enable you to live freely and happily. It is like learning a new language. Keep your heart open, let your emotions flow, and you'll learn this wonderful, new language.

Keep in mind that emotions can be lodged in your body, and they may need your conscious help to be brought up to the surface. You may not be able to identify your feelings immediately. You may feel unsettled or know that something is brewing, but you might not know what it is. This is perfectly normal. In order to help move it along, get moving *safely.* For example, you can jump up and down, perhaps shake/wring your hands, rock back and forth, punch a pillow, or even just tap one of your fingers. Whatever works *for you.* Physical motion is a great way to trigger your ability to release. If you get moving physically in some way with the intention of releasing your feelings, it can help you express yourself.

Let's go to the bathtub for further clarification. Imagine that your *unexpressed* feelings are like murky water in a bathtub. The bathtub is filled with murky water to the extent that you have unexpressed emotion. Imagine the bathtub filled to the brim (and perhaps overflowing) with murky water. The times when you feel sad and regretful about these emotions means that you have the opportunity to make peace with them. When you feel however you feel, it is just like pulling the plug and draining the bathtub of the murky water.

When the bathtub is already full, there is no room for new stuff. You *make* room in the bathtub for new water — the new experiences of fun, happiness and abundance you secretly (or not so secretly) wish for. It's okay to grieve for what you didn't get that you so desperately needed. So pulling the plug is what can happen when you're feeling sad or melancholy, in the form of shedding tears, gaining clarity, and draining the murky water from the bathtub. When you're sad, recognize that it is an opportunity. Neutralize it, acknowledge it, express it, and then release it. The more you release, the clearer the water becomes, which allows you to more fully attract and enjoy new experiences.

Another wonderful healing tool is music, which is such a great catalyst for expression. If you feel like you're on the brink of feeling but cannot release it, let music help you. Hum, sing or listen to music. Find music that matches your mood, or a song with lyrics that say what you're feeling. Let it in, then let yourself go. It's your secret, between you and you. While you're listening, be as expressive with your body as you can. Let music help you celebrate your reawakening self.

Lastly, in order for a new understanding to emerge, think of your toil, confusion, sadness or hurt as birth pangs. You are literally being reborn with new clarity and new understanding. Labor (just like when a woman is in process with giving birth to a child) is required. When you're in it, when you are in labor in this sense, rejoice because you know a breakthrough is coming. You're in the active process of peeling off a layer, as in onion skin. More self-empowerment is coming!

"Truly, it is in the darkness that one finds the light, so when we are in sorrow, then this light is nearest to us."
—Meister Eckhart

CB CB CB

Using Your Imagination

"Imagination is more important than knowledge."
—Albert Einstein

When I think about this statement, I'm guessing that Mr. Einstein reveled in questioning and exploring what is possible to discover, what is possible to create, and what we are free to question. So often we stay so enamored with physical existence that we become enslaved by it. "What is in front of me that I can perceive with one or more of my five senses is all that is real," we may believe. However, putting our *inner senses* to work — imagining, daydreaming and/or visualizing — allows us a remarkable freedom and fluidity of expression and creation.

Folks (especially us self-help people) talk about sitting quietly and visualizing or using your imagination. You may think this is stupid and the biggest waste of time. You may poo-poo the idea of using your imagination because it doesn't have anything to do with the "real" world.

Well, sorry to break the news to you, but you do use your imagination. All of the time, in fact. How often do you worry about what tragedies might befall you or your loved ones? Do you ever think about knocking somebody out? How often? Or do you worry about traffic and being late for that appointment or picking up the kids from school? Isn't *that* using your imagination?

So yes, your imagination is alive and well. It's not a matter of how to *do* it because you already do it, briefly and in spurts, every day. Now it is a matter of what you are *focusing* on when you do it. Take yourself off of automatic pilot and observe what you think about. What are the primary and continuous thoughts going through your head? Are they pleasant or full of worry? *Just observe.*

Your inner world, like your dream world, does not conform to the rules of physical reality. Time can bend, experiences can be replaced, and beliefs can shift. It's a very vibrant, dynamic landscape which you can familiarize yourself with in order to change your life. Psychologists and others have researched and worked with it for centuries, and there are countless resources to further explore the power of your inner world.

New discoveries in the form of the mind/body connection are happening all of the time. With all of the wonderful research, nothing can validate its practical and effective qualities more than using it.

It's time to see how well your imagination works. In your mind's eye, see the front door to where you live right now. What color is the door? And on what side of the door is the handle? Now open your eyes. Simply put, you have just worked with your inner world, your inner sensing. It's that simple!

CB CB CB

The Anger Release Exercise

Let's now use visualization to process emotion so that you can add it as an option alongside physically expressing yourself and expressing yourself through writing. The next exercise is also very helpful to determine if what you're feeling now has also brought up old lemons that are ready to transform. Getting a two-for-one is very exciting!

Here is the example we will use:

You and your best friend are having a private and very personal conversation. You're in a house with other people, but you and your friend are alone in a room. The door is slightly open. You're pouring your heart out and suddenly you hear someone laughing right outside the door, and you realize that someone has been listening to your private conversation. Now you're absolutely LIVID. You feel angry, embarrassed, vulnerable and humiliated. You actually want to punch them in the face.

Rather than lash out at the person, stay as calm as possible. Say very little (if anything at all) to them. Neutralize it in your head for the moment. "My friend and I were talking and some JERK was listening, and I am really upset about it." Stay furious, because that is exactly how you are feeling … do not fake or deny that. If you feel like you have to leave, do it. Take care of yourself. And as soon as you have time to be alone, here is what you do.

The Exercise[*]

- Close your eyes and breathe deeply.

- Feel yourself wrapped in a warm bubble of safety, where you are free to express yourself with harm to none.

---

[*] I recommend that you read through the exercise in its entirety at least once so that you are familiar with it before actually doing it. Once you understand the steps, you may find yourself much more relaxed when you actually do it.

- Now see the person you're upset with in your mind's eye, standing directly in front of you. Stay with it until you can see them as best you can. Don't try to be perfect. Whatever image you get is just fine.

- LET THEM HAVE IT. In your mind's eye, see yourself telling them whatever is on your mind. See yourself yelling and screaming at them, if that is how you feel. Don't sugarcoat anything. Examples: "How DARE you listen to MY conversation that has nothing to do with you?" "I have never felt more embarrassed in my life." "You have no respect for my privacy and I want to punch you in your face." Keep going until you feel like you have said everything you need to say to them.

- See the person agreeing with you. To everything you tell them, in your mind's eye, see them agreeing with you. You say, "How DARE you be in my business that has nothing to do with you?" And they respond back to you, "My goodness, I did do that, huh? You're absolutely right." You say, "You embarrassed and humiliated me," and they respond back to you, "You're absolutely right. I *did* do that, huh?"

- Continue with the back and forth dialogue. Say exactly what you need to say, and see them agree with you on EVERYTHING. Keep going until you feel that you have said everything you need to say.

- After you're done saying what you need to say, see them apologizing to you. "I am SO very sorry," they say to you. For every point you make, they acknowledge it, agree with you, and tell you that they are sorry.

- Once they apologize, see them look at you and say, "I want to make it up to you. Please tell me how I can make it up to you."

- Tell them all of the things they need to do for you in the form of positive wishes. Say things like: "I would like for you to respect my privacy" … "I would like for you to honor my feelings" … etc.

- See them smile and nod at you. Feel them give you everything that you asked for. Be still and let the good feeling wrap around you like a warm, soft blanket. Your space is respected. Your feelings are honored, etc.

- When you feel quiet and peaceful inside, give yourself permission to come back into the room, and when you are ready, open your eyes.

The point is to speak your mind, absolutely, but to do it in a different forum first — before discussing your issues with the other person. When you're alone and in a safe place, let it out — either through the anger exercise, or consciously and physically (e.g., beat on pillows, yell and scream, cuss out the person [in the privacy of your own space]). In this way, everything you feel and say is 100% acceptable and accepted, period. Do no harm to yourself or property, or others around you. That way, you can honor your anger without having to apologize to anyone about how you feel, or sabotaging your own life by getting arrested, etc. Nobody will be there disagreeing with you, or not seeing your point of view. In your own space, your point of view is totally valid and accepted. HEAR YOURSELF! Surrender to your wave of emotion. As sure as the tide hits the shore, the wave will subside. Trust that your emotions will run their course. Do not fear your energy-in-motion ... embrace it!

You can also write it out. Tell the person everything you have to say. Let it out, then express *and* receive your positive wishes. Since you have processed and released the experience (and hopefully feel better), feel free to destroy what you wrote if you wish because you don't need it anymore.

Again, the whole idea is to express what you have to express and tell the person who hurt you exactly what you want to say to them, and you are doing it in a safe, trustworthy environment. It is rarely a good idea to directly confront those who hurt us, because chances are you will be re-victimized. They may deny what you say to them ("That didn't happen"), or they might minimize what happened ("You are overreacting ... it wasn't that bad"). Well, the point is, it was bad *for you* and that is what matters. You need to find your own space where you are free to express yourself, 100%, honestly and openly, and without judgment. After you express it, and get your positive wishes from it, you start to heal on the inside, and your life changes on the outside.

As I mentioned earlier, once you completely release emotionally, you may be physically tired — which is normal. It takes a little time for your mind and body to adjust to the release. *Take care of yourself.* Acknowledge that YOU ROCK! Let your mind relax and do something you enjoy. Be patient and wait for clarity about the situation once you have released your anger.

If at some point you decide that it is necessary to address the inappropriate behavior directly with the person, you may get an apology from them, or maybe not. But once you have safely released your anger, the sting will be gone because you *got over* it. And because you have already said what you needed to say and responded to what needed healing, the other person's reaction is secondary. You run your own show. And since that situation gave you the opportunity to clear up something deeper (and you have effectively cleared out space to embrace new and preferred situations, relationships and experiences), you may feel inclined to *thank them*!

Use the "Anger Release" Exercise or offline writing exercise when you feel upset. You may also check to see if there's a deeper hurt that you now have the ability to clear out. Below are a couple of steps to add to the Anger Release Exercise to see if you're really angry with someone else (which keeps repeating itself in your life).

While you're doing the Anger Release Exercise and you're at the point where you are letting the other person have it ("How DARE you listen to MY conversation that has nothing to do with you," etc.), in your mind's eye, see the person move to the side. Is there someone standing directly behind them? If so, *that* is the actual person you are very upset with. It could be your mother or your father, or someone else from your past who really hurt you. Trust who you find behind the person. Chances are that you will recognize the connection as soon as you see them.

Let's say, for example, that it's your mother. When you were young, she never gave you privacy and was always in your business — telling you how to live and think and feel and just suffocated you in general. Now (within the Anger Release Exercise) let HER have it. Tell her exactly how you feel. The words may be exactly what you said to the first person. "How DARE you be in my business that has nothing to do with you?" "You embarrassed and humiliated me all my life." "You have no respect for my privacy and I am completely upset with you about it." Continue with the exercise by seeing her agree with you on every point. See her apologize, then let her make it up to you by receiving the positive wishes you set forth.

Your inner landscape — your conscious and subconscious mind — are amazing things. It's not necessary to clear things up with the actual person. You clear them up with yourself, through yourself. Chances are the other person will never give you what you need and want from them. They may not be present enough or caring enough or capable of doing it. Moreover, they also could no longer be on the planet. So does that make you forever stuck because you can't physically confront them? *Absolutely not.* You have the ability to free yourself from the bonds of anger and hurt without the other person being present.

Understand that when you use your imagination to visualize and work with your inner world, you actually do transform your inner world. You will feel a shift on the inside. You will feel peaceful and quiet on the inside, and hopefully many more terrific and amazing feelings!

If you're diligently working with shifting your perspective to understand the connection between your inner and outer worlds, once you begin working the Anger Release Exercise, you will experience it. It's quite profound how acknowledging a past hurt then transforming it into self-love can change your world.

The more you find yourself doing this particular exercise, the more magical your world will become. If you use nothing else, when you incorporate this exercise into your life, you are responding to previously unmet needs and your life will shift. You can use this one tool for the rest of your life and, chances are, you will need it less and less as you drain the bathtub.

Lastly, the more often you do this exercise, the more you will get used to making the connections. You will be able to cycle through the whole exercise very quickly, even in a matter of moments, to completely transform old hurts through current experiences.

Things will repeat themselves until you seize the opportunity to clear up what is truly eating at you. When you face then resolve the real hurt, you receive the gift that is intended for you, and you can get *over* it and move on. Gone will be the days of repeating the same old patterns and attracting non-preferred experiences and people. There will be no need.

Visualization processes are exactly that: *processes*. They are slow and steady. Take your time with them, one step at a time. Soon you will open up to them. It may not happen all at once, or at first, but if not don't get discouraged. Keep with it and trust your timing. Your experience is uniquely your own. Don't judge what you get or do not get. Let it be okay as it is. It can be very effective even if the images in your mind's eye come and go, or are not there at all. The point is to ride it through until the end until you feel yourself receiving the love and self-regard that you deserve.

Offline

When you're angry at someone, work with the following:

What happened?

Tell the person exactly how you feel about it. Don't sugar coat anything.

Let them apologize to you. What words of apology are they using?

Let them make it up to you. Write down your positive wishes:

"I would like for you to—," and
"I would like for you to—," and
"I would like for you to—."

Keep writing your positive wishes and feel them giving you what you ask for.

CB CB CB

Transform Your B, S, G and R

If you notice that you can't freely receive love or get what you set forth as your positive wishes, know that it is terrific that you're at least able to determine that. Don't judge it; just acknowledge it. Chances are that there are still some things that you have yet to reconcile internally that are blocking you from receiving love, and it is usually some form of blame, shame, guilt or regret. Understand that blame and shame, then guilt and regret can occur *as survival responses to your non-preferred situations, and they exist when your needs are unmet.*

If you really look at it, the typical thing we do is blame ourselves for everything bad that happens in our lives. If our parents divorce, somehow it is our fault ... we are to blame for it. If our father gets drunk and hits us or hits our brothers and sisters, or abuses our mother, we may blame ourselves for not being able to stop it and we may feel ashamed about it. If we are of mixed-heritage, we feel compromised somehow because we may not have a true identification as far as race is concerned, and straddling two can be riddled with its own challenges. When we find ourselves orphans due to war, we may blame ourselves. When we find it difficult to break the cycle of negative patterns that have been in our families for generations, we may still blame ourselves.

You may have been screamed at, bullied or beaten. You may have witnessed horrific things. Or you may have been ignored. You may have been taught that crying (or expressing anything for that matter) is bad and that having what you want is virtually impossible. We may blame ourselves for this.

Can you imagine (and do you remember) blaming yourself when you were ten for not being able to control your mother, your father, the weather or a war? It is way unfair for our precious little selves to try to figure this out or to try to handle it, but we try. As a result, we may have adopted very critical thoughts about ourselves and others. We adopt these habits when we are young, and as we grow, we may unconsciously block our ability to receive love.

When you were young, if you experienced traumatic and/or hurtful experiences and were not able to release the shock, or cry when you were hurt then be comforted, your needs were unmet. Because your needs were unmet, chances are that you began acting in ways in response to your unmet needs that you were not proud of — thus the onset of guilt and regret. When you were unable to understand or express your emotions in a healthy manner, they may have turned into anger or apathy or depression — among other things.

In anger, we can act out against ourselves and/or others (usually those less likely to fight back), and both become more wounded. If we believe that these are not good things to do, guilt and/or regret can result. With apathy, we may numb out, shut down and pretend that we don't care. Depression happens when we focus on our non-preferred situations and feel helpless to make any type of positive change.

Throughout the ages, it has been said that our essence is love. We are born knowing what love feels like. As children, we are open and loving. We smile at strangers before we are taught differently (and, unfortunately, appropriately so).

As children, we may become familiar with disillusionment because we know what love is supposed to look like. When we experience something SO different, we can be traumatized.

"Wait," we think (or even say), "if you loved me, you wouldn't be doing this ..." All because we know what love feels like when we feel it.

Therefore, consider this: *the issues you face and the ways that you reacted are in direct response to the lack of love.* The lack of love is what you responded to.

Feelings of unworthiness can be habitual and deeply embedded. You may feel that, even now, no matter how good things may *appear* to be, someday soon it will all come crashing down. We can be very diligent about waiting for the other shoe to drop. But let this be the other shoe to drop: *now* is the time to acknowledge and honor what you had to do to survive, then let it go.

The point here is to shift your perception on your blame, shame and guilt and regret altogether. It's now time to focus on honoring what you had to do to survive. How did you adapt to your situation? What did you adopt as your survival mechanisms?

If you cannot think about these things in terms of yourself personally, that is quite all right. Think about a child, any child, experiencing what you went through, and doing what you did in response to it. Was he or she in a position to really understand what was happening around them and to them? Was he or she in a position to change the beliefs and behaviors of those around them? *No!*

Use neutralization for help with stopping self-judgment or self-blame over what happened so you can express your honest sadness or grief. Beating yourself up as an automatic response prevents you from the healthy releasing that can help you get over hurts from the past.

Offline

What happened?

Did you blame yourself? If yes, why?

What did you do as a result of blaming yourself?

Do you still feel guilty about it? Describe it.

What did you really want instead of what you got?

Is there anyone who you would like to apologize to?

Is there anything else on your mind that you want to talk about?

CB CB CB

For your very survival, you may have adapted to what was going on around you by covering up your sensitivity. The name of the game may have been to appear as strong as possible; to pretend that you are not vulnerable. You pretend to be someone else other than your true self in order to survive and to minimize the amount of hurt you may feel.

*"There is a secret person undamaged
in every individual."*

—Paul Shepard

The part of you that knows what love is still lives within you. It may be buried underneath all of the pain, unexpressed hurt and our habitual pretending to be someone else, but that inner knowingness never dies. It is always with you. It originates beyond your body. It is eternal.

As you learn to respond to your unmet needs, blame and shame can be replaced with feelings of absolute worthiness. Consider that young ones whose emotional needs are met are blameless, shameless, and guilt-free because there is no need for those feelings.

Guilt and regret are debts that can never be repaid. No matter what you do or don't do, they will always demand more from you. The more you do to respond to them, the more they will expect you to pay.

ଔ ଔ ଔ

The Guilt/Regret Exercise

To better respond to an experience for which you harbor guilt and/or regret, here is an exercise that you can use to transform it. First, use the "what happened" from the offline writing you just did. Recall how old you were at that time (it could have happened yesterday or decades ago, and for this purpose it is a "younger you").

The Exercise

*(Remember to read through the exercise thoroughly
at least once so that you understand what it entails.)*

- Close your eyes and breathe deeply.

- Feel yourself wrapped in a warm bubble of safety, where you are free to express yourself with harm to none.

- Now see the younger you appear before you. (Stay with it until you can see him/her as best you can. Don't try to be perfect. Whatever image you get is just fine. Are you sitting across from each other at a table? Are you both standing? Are the two of you sitting on the floor with legs crossed?)

- Neutralize your judgment as you ask the younger you to talk about what happened. Allow a dialogue between the two of you to occur. Feel compassion as your younger you expresses how they feel about his/her choices.

- Once your younger self expresses all he/she needs to express, offer him/her your forgiveness. Help them understand that they were acting from hurt and pain at the time ... that it wasn't their fault; that they did the best they could with what they knew at the time. Feel free to open up and be really specific with them about what happened and how they are not to be blamed. Beam out forgiveness to them. Wrap them in compassion and understanding.

- See your younger self ask for forgiveness from the people who may have been hurt by their actions.

- Ask your younger self what they would do differently if they could do it over again. Allow them to do the event over again and make a different choice, one that has a new and happy ending. As you both witness the happy ending, see the scene fade away. Both of you say farewell to it and release the event from your life.

- Ask your younger self for forgiveness for judging and condemning him/her for so long. Give them whatever time he or she may need to really accept forgiving you, then see him/her forgiving you.

- Look into each other's eyes with understanding, forgiveness and support. Give your younger self a big and reassuring hug. See them hug you back and then smile at you. Give him or her a gift, something that they would like, such as their favorite toy or game, before you tell them good-bye.

- When you feel quiet and peaceful inside, give yourself permission to come back into the room. When you are ready, open your eyes.

After doing this exercise, you may experience a definite shift when you do the Anger Release exercise again. When it's time to imagine receiving your positive wishes, you'll have likely moved into a feeling of deservability which will allow you to receive what you want.

Use this exercise with as many guilt/regret experiences as you encounter. Remember that sometimes a more recent version of yourself will appear across from you and not necessarily your child self.

As you develop your new practice of self-forgiveness and release shame and regret, the practice can become a guide in helping you discover ways to serve others. With healthy remorse, you may find yourself wanting to help others — not from a repayment of guilt perspective but from a healed, service-oriented, genuine desire to help. You can be most effective in service when you bring the *real* you to the table!

Ↄ Ↄ Ↄ

Pep Talk #2

When you continue to transform your inner world, other experiences may come to mind that you will want to make sure receive healing as well. Do the exercises over and over again. *Keep healing!* By acknowledging, transforming, and then releasing whatever comes up, you give yourself the ability to live firmly in the present so that you can create the life you wish to live.

At the same time, don't think that you somehow have to identify and clear up *all* of your beliefs and/or non-preferred situations in order to live your most fabulous life. Quite the opposite! However, if many of your non-preferred situations are gone and/or already forgotten, *good*. But know that you have the ability to attract abundance in spite of that old stuff.

Once you begin to feel empowered by the way you are responding to your life's challenging experiences, you will enjoy a profound sense of freedom. By reading this book, you now know how to add water to your lemons. You can now move from living in fear to flowing with your life; no matter what comes up, you know how to process it.

Gone are the days of trying to change other people so that you can feel better. *Gone* are the days of needing to see your value and worth in the eyes of another first. *Gone* are the days of feeling helpless and unable to respond to the challenges in your life. As you shift your perspective, you understand that your challenges are really opportunities to heal and honor yourself. *You can get over it!* You have the ability, here and now, to transform your life. Have the willingness, use these tools, and get ready to soar!

"There's only one corner of the universe you can be certain of improving, and that's your own self."

—Aldous Huxley

Sugar

To Have and To Hold

Here comes the fun part where you will explore freedom and love. They are both yours to have and to hold forever!

Let's start with a famous scene from the movie *Casablanca*. Humphrey Bogart (as Rick Blaine) sees Ingrid Bergman (as Ilsa Lund, his former lover) walk into his bar during World War II, and he thinks about the fact that out of all the places in the world it was his "gin joint" that she entered.

Imagine the endless number of possibilities of the experiences you could have had. Think about all of the places in the world you could have been born. Consider each day, each month, each decade and each century in relation to the actual date and time of your birth. Consider your parents. Imagine all of the people you could encounter, all of the qualities you could possess, or the infinite number of experiences you could have had. And from all of those possibilities, you were born where you were born, you think how you think, and you are who you are. Your family, social and cultural background are what they are. You have encountered the people you have encountered.

Given all that *could have* occurred, and given what *did* occur, wouldn't it make sense that what you experienced is uniquely yours? That it really and truly belongs to you? This would also imply that since you're the one doing the experiencing, you are responsible for it. Remember that responsibility simply means having the ability to respond.

Perhaps you have heard the phrase, "You are not given more than you can handle." Is this statement, considering the actual events that have taken place in your life (in light of all of the possibilities), something that you are willing to consider? If so, then perhaps it is also appropriate to consider the idea that there are no accidents in your life; that instead there are opportunities to learn and to thrive within *everything* that you encounter.

Consider that your plate of lemons is PERFECT for you! They don't belong to your friends, family members or colleagues; they are *uniquely yours*.

When you move forward with the understanding that: (1) your lemons are *your* lemons, (2) they serve you somehow, and (3) you have the ability to respond to them, *be prepared to triumph*. If you believe that your non-preferred situations serve you somehow, you are able to live in the present without fear of what is to come. If the future holds something that is non-preferred, you will already know how to respond to it; therefore it's no longer non-preferred and everything becomes a party!

With your new outlook, be prepared to experience some "cosmic hugs" as a by-product. "Cosmic hugs" come in the form of unexpected luck — such as a chance meeting that is really beneficial to you in some way, or even running out of gas as soon as you pull up to the pump. Your new outlook will open up wonderful possibilities for you, simply because you shifted your thinking. Your acknowledgement of the cosmic hugs invites them to keep happening. Even when you cannot identify them, just keep moving forward.

Here's a perfect example of a shift in mindset when you embrace your lemons and know that there's something good in it for you. When something non-preferred happens, say to yourself, "I *meant* to do that!" Of course, you may not know *why* you "meant" to do it, but that will be yours to discover and understand in your own timing.

I'm not making light of your lemons, and especially not the real impactful ones. In fact, I'd bet the farm that there's no way a rape victim would say, "I *meant* to do that!" The truth is that when you're victimized, you're PISSED, HURT, DEVASTATED, SHOCKED … fill in the blank … all feelings are appropriate. But through the gift of time and inner work (i.e., adding water to lemons), the rape *victim* can transform into the rape *survivor.*

The rape survivor might tell you that because of being raped he or she accessed inner strength that they didn't know they had. He or she might tell you that they learned to protect himself/herself. They might tell you that they no longer fear the future because he or she believes that after surviving it and ultimately thriving, they are able to survive and then thrive after *any* circumstance. That even if he or she could change it, they wouldn't because of the value received as a result of it. He or she may go as far as to say that being raped lead to a very important and necessary course correction in their life that guided them to the life they intended to live. *This all is possible.* The path has already been paved in this way because there's at least one survivor who can attest to this.

☙ ☙ ☙

Perception: Your Ultimate Freedom

Simply put, what you *believe* about what you *perceive* is what you will *receive.* In this regard, the following quote is much more eloquent:

> *"Your living is determined not so much by what life brings to you as by the attitude you bring to life; not so much by what happens to you as by the way your mind looks at what happens."*

—Khalil Gibran

Whatever is real in your head makes it real in "real life." If you're looking for a fight, you will certainly find one. If you constantly observe people, things and events with the intention of finding something wrong, you will, most assuredly, find something wrong. Conversely, if you look for things that are working, you will receive confirmation that there are some things that are indeed working. Both are correct because we are (each and individually) doing the perceiving. Whether you see the glass as half empty or half full, your life will support your assumption. *Either way, you are right!*

Have you ever been in a situation with someone else where you both witness the same event yet the two of you see it differently? You may think, "How can they possibly see it that way?" Yet the other person is as correct as you are because we look at everything through the lens of our own background, culture, experiences and beliefs. Again, whatever you believe about what you perceive is how it will impact you. The world will look how you say it will look.

For example, why do you go to work every day? You may think about things like paying your bills, having a sense of integrity, etc. But if you shifted it to think about what you are able to enjoy because of going to work, your answer might change. So let's try that question again! Why do you go to work every day? You go to work every day because you see a cute dress that you want to buy, or there's a movie playing that you want to check out this weekend. Yes, your work enables you to keep the lights on, but it also helps you do things that you enjoy.

Your mind is the place where life can shift. Once you get comfortable with the fact that you think in all different kinds of ways, you can become more skilled at focusing your attention. Your mind is like a wild horse — it performs better when tamed.

> *"We don't see things as they are,*
> *we see them as we are."*
>
> —Anais Nin

To go a step further, imagine that the world isn't a foreign place that you were born into, but rather that it's more like your personal "gin joint" — the playing field *you* create in order to learn to focus your thoughts. What you believe in your heart of hearts is what you will manifest. No amount of positive thinking will overtake that which you believe (or fear) the most. This is why doing the water work is so important because you tell yourself your absolute truth about everything, and that is when you have the ability to transform it. As a result, you can move from hoping you get what you want into knowing that you can create what you want, and this happens from the *inside* out. From there, it can be a tremendously interesting and fun journey.

Quantum physicists have explored the scientific validity of *consciousness* creating form (rather than form creating consciousness) for almost a century now. The hypotheses and material on this subject are immense. From the initial works of pioneers like Max Planck, Max Born, Niels Bohr, Erwin Schrodinger and Werner Heisenberg, to today's groundbreakers (e.g., David Gross, Bertrand Halperin, Ian Thompson and Amit Goswami), there is great support to embrace such a radical paradigm shift.

Therein lays your ultimate freedom. You have the innate ability to change your mind about something. You can shift your thinking at will. You may initially see something as a challenge; however the moment you view it as an opportunity, your reality changes because *you* will have changed. From there springs your own creativity to enjoy life as you wish. Use your imagination to find new and empowering ways to look at things.

For example, you get a flat tire after heading out one morning. You're completely annoyed because the flow of your day is already interrupted. You decide to fix it yourself, and while you're fixing it, you contemplate how the flat tire serves you. You're still annoyed about it and don't want to think about any of that airy fairy stuff right now. But you decide to trust that it serves you somehow, even if you don't know how at the moment. With that thought, you find that your mood changes. You're no longer as annoyed as you were. You decide to neutralize it ("I got a flat tire") and continue your day.

The next morning, you stop at the cleaners to drop off the pants that you dirtied while fixing your flat tire. While in the cleaners, someone parks their car next to yours. When you go outside, you cannot believe what you see. You have been looking for your dream car, a 1966 Mustang. But you haven't had any luck because you would need a true fixer-upper in order to be able to afford it. The car is even the color that you imagined. Lo and behold, there is a "for sale" sign inside, and it's even within your price range!

Many times, people have the opportunity to say, "If it wasn't for X, I wouldn't have Y." Oftentimes the understanding comes in retrospect. Therefore, in the meantime, might it be a good thing to trust that your experiences serve you somehow (even if just for the benefit of feeling better at the moment)?

✎ **Offline** ✎

Pick one of your non-preferred experiences.

What happened?

How did you view it at the time?

Looking at it in retrospect, how did it serve you exactly as it was? What do you now understand because of it?

C8 C8 C8

A Puzzle for Game Lovers

It's time to begin connecting the dots. Your life experiences tell a story. It is like a puzzle that you can put together to get a fuller picture. You may now get a deeper understanding of yourself by observing patterns or consistent trends in your life. Practice observing them in terms of *themes*. Put together the puzzle pieces of your life.

Here are a few examples that may offer clues to your own patterns. From them, you may be able to start to identify aspects of your journey that you can work with. The first column shows what you may have experienced, the next column shows how you may have responded to what happened, and the third column shows what can result during your journey of healing.

What Happened	Your Response	Your Healed State
Abandonment	Abandon others / Others abandoning you; Short-term relationships, lack or loss of friends	Allowing committed relationships / Being committed to others
Abuse (i.e., Betrayal of Trust)	Betray others' trust; Others betray you; Lying, stealing, cheating	Being trustworthy
Being Misunderstood	Instigator of problems, Manipulation, Lying	Being understanding
Victimization	Victimize yourself (drugs / alcohol / cutting, etc.) and/or Victimize others	Protector / Healer

Here's another way to make the connection between lemons and lemonade. Consider why retail stores hire former shoplifters as part of their security team. The ideal folks to assist someone with an alcohol issue are sometimes those of us who are recovering substance abusers. A survivor of abuse may have a gift of knowing what to say to comfort abused children. Your patterns may hold the clues to how you can serve others in the future.

There are, of course, other themes to consider; however when it comes to lemons, these four — abandonment, abuse, misunderstanding and victimization — are common. If you're stumped as to where your themes are with the following offline exercise, that is quite all right. If you keep writing, you will receive some clarity on it at some point. If you don't, then trust that it is for your own good reason and keep moving forward anyway.

Offline

Start with information about your lemons. Describe what happened. As you recount your lemons, see if you can detect a pattern. Is there a continuous theme of abandonment? Abuse? Feeling left out? Loneliness? Being misunderstood?

When you observe what happened, allow your emotions to flow should your writing trigger something. It's a tremendous opportunity to address this so that it can transform. Use the techniques you are now familiar with: cry, beat on pillows, yell, write, visualize. Let it flow. Allow your different voices to have their say if they indeed want to express about it. See those who wronged you apologize to you for their shortcomings and for your pain. Set forth your positive wishes and imagine receiving them. Keep your nurturer in the mix as well. Reinforce your value to yourself. Tell your little one how much you love them; that things were not their fault and that you are there to protect and love them. Take your time with this. Stay with it until you surrender to a feeling of peace (or a quiet mind).

Write out the following: "I am willing to release the pattern of _____ in my life. I am willing to forgive myself for all that happened because of it. I am willing to release it now."

Once you feel complete with your willingness to release it, write about what you will now attract into your life. Dream big! Imagine what you want; now imagine it already with you. How do you feel now that it's here? See it in your mind. Use your senses to make it come alive. In your mind, touch it, smell it, feel it, taste it. Fill your senses with all of the good feelings you have now that it's in your life.

Once you feel nice and full and happy, is there anything else on your mind that you want to talk about?

⌘ ⌘ ⌘

Puzzle #2 – More Information

*"One generation opens the road upon which
another generation travels."*

—Chinese Proverb

Another impactful area to reflect upon is your own heritage and background. They certainly contribute to you being who you are. You might understand more about yourself and your unique opportunities by taking a look at the challenges that your ancestors faced.

For example, let's say that your great grandmother, grandmother *and* mother were all single mothers who sacrificed to provide for their families. Do you think that they would prefer that you be bitter and angry about the fact that they raised their families alone? Or do you think that they would prefer that you honor and appreciate their sacrifice by creating a happy and empowered life for yourself?

Let's say that because of your family background, you are especially sensitive to the idea of single parenthood. Part of your empowered state may be to stop that cycle within your own family by working at all times to maintain a healthy marriage. Or you may feel compelled to become an educator with emphasis on ideas that promote and support family unity.

Also consider the resilience it took for them to ensure the survival of their children, which, in turn, ensured your survival as well. The love, strength, courage and steadfastness of your ancestors flow through your veins. It is embedded in your DNA. The best of them lives within you. Call upon those virtues to motivate you in your own life, and imagine them cheering you on as you align yourself with them. Living your best life honors *them*.

Take it one step further by imagining the help they had that allowed them to raise their family. Assistance may have come in the form of extended family and even strangers who offered a helping hand along the way. Acknowledge all of these unsung heroes for enabling you to exist. Their sacrifice is a profound testimony to the value of your life.

Offline #1

Identify a challenge that your ancestors faced.

List some of the qualities you think they would have had to have in order to survive.

Acknowledge these qualities in them and express your appreciation for them.

"I appreciate you for—"
"I appreciate you for—"
"I appreciate you for—"
"I appreciate you for—"

If your ancestors could speak to you right now, what words of encouragement do you imagine that they would say to you?

Now re-read the words of encouragement that you just wrote and let them in even more.

✎ Offline #2 ✎

Where does your family come from?

What are some of the characteristics of that culture that you can identify with?

Can you see any parallels to your own life? If so, what are they?

What value have these parallels brought to your life?

Consider this ... whatever your thoughts, feelings, experiences and background have been, they were 100% tailor-made *just for you*. It's wrapped in divine wisdom to suit your own higher purpose and holds magnificent gifts and growth opportunities for you. If there is a thought or idea that you find intriguing about your heritage and/or background, it's your indicator as to what you may want to explore about your own life's patterns and/or themes. It can provide clues as to what you can seek to clear up.

You can do inner world exercises at anytime you wish in order to send gratitude, forgiveness and compassion to an entire culture, a historical event, a family member, etc. The results may also be an indicator of that which excites you, as well as certain traits and latent abilities within yourself that you may wish to explore and develop.

ೞ ೞ ೞ

Love: The Final Frontier

And, finally, let's talk about love.

When you find that you're acknowledged, understood, safe and valued, you might not necessarily think that this is a bad thing — would you?

Here are some thoughts about what love is:

- Receiving acknowledgment
- Receiving understanding
- Feeling safe
- Being treated kindly, in words and in deeds
- Feeling valued
- Lightness and fun
- Being adored

Many of the ways that you respond to others (and they to you) are about seeking acknowledgment and wanting to be understood. If you look around, we interact with each other in an attempt to be loved, or else our behavior reflects what happens when we don't have the love that we need.

All this time, you may have been searching for love in other people. So often others can fall short of meeting your needs and expectations. This isn't necessarily because they don't care, but because they are doing the best they can as well, and may not have it to give (at least not in the way that *you* want it).

Is it even possible for someone else to peer into your soul, completely understand you, and give you exactly what you need at all times? Is it possible to find someone who will acknowledge, understand and value you unconditionally, and always at the perfect time and right on the mark?

Are you even willing to receive it? Perhaps after having experienced lemons in that department, you may have your heart under lock and key for self-preservation, and understandably so. You are not alone. You may be familiar with the dance: "If you acknowledge, understand and value me *first*, then I will feel better about you and can be more loving towards you." In turn your friend may say, "Well, if *you* love *me*, then I will feel better about you and can give *you* the love that you need." Here is where we become ultra polite, as if opening a door for someone. "You go first." "No, that's okay, *you* go first." "If *you* go first, *then* I'll go." In other words, show me that you love me first, and then I will return the love.

But while you contemplate things, you are still falling short of what you need when it comes to love.

If you were able to ask Leonardo Del Vecchio, Carly Simon, or Oprah how they were able to achieve what they did, I would be willing to bet that you would find that love was (and continues to be) part of the equation.

Acknowledgement, understanding, self-value, safety, fun, laughter and being utterly adored are yours to have. If you are breathing, you deserve it. It is simple as that.

All the exercises, information and suggestions I provide are designed to assist you in your willingness and ability to receive love. Inside of you is where your true home is, and the intention is for love to reach you, even just a little bit, and however it may come. Whether it comes through your front door, the back door, a side door, a window or a crack in the floor, if something clicks that is the whole point.

Every facet of your being yearns for love. The deepest recesses of your being yearn for acknowledgement and understanding. It is time to reawaken to that which is your birthright. Love is the sugar. Receiving love is the third and final ingredient needed to make lemonade.

How do you attract love into your life? How do you receive acknowledgment, understanding and a sense of value from others? You do it by cultivating it yourself, on the inside first. Once you make the connection, it is permanent. It is the most incredible and freeing experience. I will share with you how I was able to make the connection.

First and foremost, this is your secret. It is between you and yourself. Nobody else has to know what you are doing. This is true offline stuff. You can explore this very, very safely and with great results!

Before we get into the "how-to," let's take a look at what you have to look forward to. The love I am talking about for you will be *unconditional*. You will be able to receive it *at will*. You will feel understood, safe and absolutely adored. It will be exactly what you want and need. And, again, once you make the connection, it will be permanent.

From there, you will be able to manifest your dreams more quickly, and they can be even bigger than you had imagined. Your relationships will shift because you will have made a shift. Things you may have yearned for can naturally happen. You have the ability to feel so adored that you may no longer be attached to getting what you thought you wanted otherwise. Then you become free to explore even more!

You will know what being loved feels like. If you already know what it feels like, that is terrific! Let's get you even more love and make your life even sweeter than it already is!

CB CB CB

Love: Fill in the Gaps

Why are we equipped with imagination and awareness of that beyond our five senses if we're not supposed to use it to our advantage? What would be the point otherwise?

*"Love makes up for the lack of long memories
by a sort of magic. All other affections need a past:
Love creates a past which envelops us,
as if by enchantment."*

—Benjamin Constant Adolphe

Now it's time to bend time. Allow yourself to consider that time is not linear; that when you think of something from your past, you can still change it. You can use your imagination to change it so that you feel good about it right now. This sounds counter-intuitive; however, when you are committed and actually do it often, you will know, firsthand, that it works.

It's time to nurture yourself. It's time to send love to every part of you and in every phase and aspect of your life. The practice of nurturing may be unfamiliar, especially if you didn't receive much of it while growing up. However, with commitment, it can be learned. Know that this is your way out of despair and your way into the life greater than your dreams. If the idea of nurturing yourself is a bit heavy to wrap your arms around, the practice of giving yourself *attention* works. If we break down the idea/definition of attention, what does that really mean? Giving attention means to simply be interested in something and acknowledge that it exists.

Every time you think of yourself as a child, shower your little one with gifts. For example, if your little one wanted to have a close relationship with your mom and it was simply not like that while you were growing up, give it to your little one right now. See your little one doing the special and fun activities with Mom that they always wanted to do.

Let's say that you played sports as a kid and, for whatever reason, your mother rarely or never came to your games and that really hurt your feelings. Now that *you* are the parent, give your little one what they want. Close your eyes and see yourself as a child playing sports. See your mother in the stands or on the sidelines smiling, cheering and clapping for you. Feel her love and support … see yourself playing better than ever! See her hug you after the game with joy, or truly comforting you if you didn't do as well as you wanted to do. But see yourself really kicking butt and having a terrific time. And see your mother sharing it with you.

Maybe you didn't grow up with your father and have always longed for a relationship with him. Give it to yourself now. Your little one has the ability to be whole and complete and receive everything they may have lacked. *Be creative.* Imagine your father happily and joyfully being with you: taking you to the park; talking to you about the birds and bees; telling you that you look breathtaking in your prom dress; or teaching you how to tie your first necktie. See him reveling in all your successes and cheering you on as you take on new challenges. Make it as big and as rich and wonderful as you can imagine.

As you incorporate these inner-world healing exercises into your life, incorporate more and more fun, nurturing and/or relaxing activities into your outer world as well. Get into some real "turn off your brain" fun. Specific relaxation activities are things like taking a relaxing bath/shower, napping more often if you can, dancing or writing. Enjoy sports, hiking, walking in nature, running, going to an amusement park or attending an outdoor event. Unleash your creativity by writing silly poetry, a short story, a fun rap song, or by drawing, painting, sculpting, sewing, etc. Laugh. Listen to music that's fun and uplifting. Sing and dance. Give yourself permission to let loose. Give yourself permission to daydream. It will feel better and better to feel good and learn to be good to yourself. Soon it will be as automatic as breathing.

As you continue to do the inner world exercises, you can quickly and effortlessly beam love to your little one during the course of your day. Continue to nurture them in this way and watch your reality transform. You may find yourself no longer focusing on finding your magical long-term relationship because you already live in a state of belonging and acceptance. When this is the case, you will have the ability to naturally attract a quality relationship from your wonderful and newly developed state of being.

ଔ ଔ ଔ

Unconditional Love: It's All Yours!

If you find that you're now getting more comfortable with your offline writing and expression, chances are you're feeling more comfortable in your own skin. *Imagine that!* You are learning to embrace more of who you truly are with less judgment and/or apology. You're feeling more relaxed as you greet each day because you are now more skilled at converting non-preferred situations (if they even arise!) to preferred situations that you can embrace. You're finding yourself more in the moment, and perhaps are experiencing more optimism and wonder. You may find yourself feeling "lighter," dreaming bigger, and bursting with new ideas and heightened creativity.

You may notice that things that used to bother you don't impact you the same. You may find your relationships shifting in unanticipated and amazing ways. You may find others commenting on there being something different about you. *Enjoy it!* Wherever you are in your process, you're on your way! It's by peeling off those first pesky layers of self-judgment, guilt and shame that you pave the way to receiving the love you need and the life that you want and so richly deserve.

You've got what you need to make lemonade: lemons, water and sugar. If you really want to go for broke, ask yourself this important question: *How much love can you handle?* Are you willing to receive more love than you could have ever imagined? Are you open to going beyond the boundaries of your understanding of love? Are you willing to receive unconditional love?

Throughout the ages, scientists, philosophers, the faithful and seekers alike have fervently explored the idea that our human essence exists *prior* to birth; that a vast and loving energy that transcends the boundaries of human existence creates us and envelops us at all times. Many writings suggest that from the moment we are born, we yearn for a loving connection that exists beyond perception, and within that understanding lies our quest to reconnect with that from which we came.

Looking back at my childhood, I remember that I felt like a fish out of water — like a foreigner in a strange and unfamiliar land. I didn't have a sense of belonging and I yearned to belong to something and/or someone who would love and adore me. I needed to know that I was special and deserving, and that no matter what I did or didn't do, they'd still love me. As long as I can remember, I searched for it. When I searched for it in other people, I came up empty-handed and disappointed every time. People were kind and all, yet what I most yearned for I couldn't verbalize, describe or find.

I came to understand that love is abundantly available to us to feel and share with each other. However, I believe that the *unconditional love* we seek in another is impossible to obtain. The reason for this is that the human experience will always be bound by time and space and circumstance. It's beyond challenging to find that which is eternal and unconditional within a system that is finite and conditional.

I believe that love — in its purest form and the way that we yearn for it — is beyond the boundaries of our human world. Yet it is still available. Our five senses are designed to perceive physical events, and our imagination is the doorway through which we can travel to perceive what is *unseen*. The unconditional love that you may yearn for is available to you. It is bigger than you are, and it's more vast and deep than any human being is able to contain or emulate. It envelops you. You just need to be willing to open your heart and mind in order to perceive *and* receive it.

This bigger love — which is beyond the boundaries of our human world — is so often attributed to the idea of the existence of a Supreme Being, or Prime Mover, or God, a Power that loves you that is bigger than you. You may already identify with sacred writings and activities in a particular way when it comes to understanding God. You may have been taught that expressing gratitude for your life and offering gratitude to God and praising God is the way to go. I certainly agree. However, feeling and expressing love and gratitude can be like a revolving door. If God is the Source of everything — an unlimited source of love — then the more you draw from that well of love, the more it becomes available to you. Certainly give and express your gratitude to God, but also *allow God's love to come TO you as well.* And to allow it to come closer and pierce that illusory veil between you, be willing to consider God *your unseen friend.*

Perhaps you may wrestle with the idea of there even *being* a God, or perhaps you are somewhere in-between. Whatever is the case for you, you are still able to connect with (or reconnect with or enhance your connection with) a never-ending source of love — *if you are willing.* In the desire to facilitate an even more personal connection, think of the idea of *unseen* — that which you can't perceive with your five senses. If you're willing, be willing to imagine that there is someone you cannot see who loves you. While this concept can be a stretch, I still present these ideas with the desire to facilitate an even deeper connection of love for you. I want to make this experience of love *very* warm and personal for you — for it to not just be a concept that you embrace, but that you really feel *how loved* you are. So to that end, I am introducing (drum roll, please) ... *your unseen friend(s).*

Of all my healing endeavors, the relationship I have come to develop with my unseen friends continues to be my foundation and mainstay for balance, understanding and my ability to express love. I wish the same for you: to know and understand with every fiber of your being how special and deserving you are, and that you are loved beyond your wildest imagination. That you are able to freely love others while you have a safe and reliable reservoir of love you can access at *any time* to replenish yourself. Again, how much love can *you* handle?

Here's where we will begin:

"God made Truth with many doors
to welcome every believer who knocks on them."

—Khalil Gibran

First, *be willing* to receive God's love. If you find the idea of receiving God's love too challenging or simply unimaginable, that's okay. Think of that which loves beyond condition and we will call them your *unseen friend(s)*. Your unseen friend may be one you may have learned about, grown up with, or constantly pray to, such as one of the following:

- Your Guardian Angel
- The Prince of Peace
- The Son of God
- The Glory of God
- The Holy Spirit
- The Enlightened One
- The Faithful One
- The Mystery of God

Pick whomever you already have a connection with from the list and be willing to have a deeper relationship with them.

If you don't have an established connection with an unseen friend such as this, that's okay. Take some time to think of someone you love who is no longer physical. Again, we're talking about love beyond the physical realm. Consider that just because your loved one died doesn't mean that they aren't still with you, loving you and cheering for you. Consider that because they are no longer constrained by a physical body, they are now free to love you in a *bigger* way. Imagine that they are still with you. Be willing to connect with them to receive their love. Pick a special person from your life to be your first unseen friend and develop a relationship with them. Perhaps it's one of the following people:

- Your Grandparent
- Your Parent, Aunt or Uncle
- Your Child
- A family member you may have never met but heard about and feel a connection to

If you cannot think of someone from your life to connect with, that's okay too. Take some time to think of an historical figure that has qualities that you respect and admire. Perhaps you share those same qualities, or aspire to have them. If you feel a connection to them somehow, be willing to develop a relationship with them. Here are some examples:

- Gandhi
- Mother Teresa
- Martin Luther King, Jr.

The key word is *relationship*. You will use your imagination to develop a relationship with them. The relationship will become as close as you allow.

Relationships take time, intention and energy to cultivate. Be willing to go beyond the world and life that you know to incorporate a new and very personal relationship with one who is willing to love you *unconditionally* — that is, your unseen friend. In fact, consider that so many have sacrificed their very lives to be of service to you in some way. They are dying to serve you and to love you. *Let them.*

You may feel a sense of embarrassment about this entire idea. That's okay. This is your secret. Be *willing* to receive your unseen friend's love. Surrendering to it can be a true challenge because you have to turn inward to get through your self-judgment in order to receive it. Be willing to let yourself go and surrender to the idea of being *adored by them.* What may initially seem unreal and unattainable can take root and have profound impact on your life. If you're willing, be willing. If you're resistant or opposed to this concept, simply be willing to consider that you are unconditionally loved, and continue to make lemonade!

Offline

Listen to at least one of the following songs. When you listen to it, imagine that your unseen friend is singing it directly to you. Know that they are sincere and singing *to you and only you.* They want to love you. *Let them.* Be willing to receive their love.

- "Baby, Baby" (written by Amy Grant and Keith Thomas, performed by Amy Grant)
- "Bridge over Troubled Water" (written by Paul Simon, performed by Simon and Garfunkel)
- "From the Bottom of My Heart" (written and performed by Stevie Wonder)
- "You Are So Beautiful" (written by Billy Preston and Bruce Fisher, performed by Joe Cocker)
- "You've Got a Friend" (written and performed by Carole King)
- "Whenever Wherever Whatever" (written and performed by Maxwell)

(And by the way, if you feel really good when you hear it, put it in your iPod today. In fact, start a playlist of love songs that you enjoy and make them all about you.)

Listen to it as often as possible. Notice that when you feel a little shy or a bit ridiculous, you're on the right track! It actually means that you're opening your heart to receive your unseen friend's love.

Ask your unseen friend to assist you in feeling the love. Keep listening to the love songs. Be willing to open up to this in your offline time.

It's time to feel love now. Make it personal, *very personal.* Someone you can't see loves you and is now able to share it with you. They are dying to be of service to you. And the variable is *you!* They are available to love *you* at all times; therefore they can love you whenever you allow them to do so.

Using this technique to access unconditional love is like having an internal valve for receiving love, like the way a water hose valve controls how much water comes out. Or perhaps an even better analogy is breath control. It's like controlling your breathing. You control how much oxygen you let into your body. When you take short breaths, you inhale small amounts of oxygen. With deeper breaths, you receive more oxygen.

So imagine them beaming love to you and sustain it as long as you can, softly and gently — like breathing. And try this from time to time … the more fully you focus on your breath, however shallow or deep, is the amount of love you can let in at that moment.

This will be an ongoing relationship, and again, you control it (as to how much you are *willing* to receive the love). Take a moment to imagine that you are a mother who loves her child (which may be the closest thing to unconditional love that we have). Now take it a step further by imagining that your unseen friend loves *you* in the same way that a mother loves her child. Yes, someone loves you in that way — *unconditionally.*

As you develop the relationship, start with honesty. Tell your truth to your unseen friend as you address your lemons.

Stop trying to be so strong in order to hold things together, and instead surrender to their love. Sure it can be scary to do the necessary lemonade work because the last thing we want to do is turn inward to face some old, painful stuff. *But the way out is in.* The old stuff will keep manifesting in your life until you address it anyway. And underneath that darkness within you, underneath that sludge (which is in the form of your unmet needs) is your freedom … your pure heart … your creative and magical self, waiting to come out and play. You may have heard the phrase, "It's never too late to have a happy childhood." Well, it really is true and the feeling of connecting to the love, abundance and joy defies imagination.

Let down your self-judgment and tell the truth to your unseen friend. Give them all of it. If on one level you are upset with "the powers that be," express it. Your friend already knows how you feel anyway. That will be how you'll get through your pain. Let the truth and the tears flow, and forge that bond with your unseen friend. Call on them to love and nurture you when you do your inner world exercises.

Remember that this is a relationship. Yell and scream at your unseen friend if and when you feel it is necessary. Let him or her apologize to you for your pain and suffering. Let him or her hold you while you cry and scream, if you wish. Remember that your thoughts and feelings are like clouds in the sky. When they are allowed to express themselves, they will naturally shift.

Again, the way out is in. The relationship is your secret. Nobody else has to know about it; it is *your* unconditionally loving relationship that you are developing.

Einstein's words are worth repeating: "Imagination is more important than knowledge." Be willing to imagine that despite your background, experiences, shortcomings and/or mistakes, your unseen friend loves you from the top of your head to the bottom of your feet. Your unseen friend worships the ground that you walk on. They adore every cell of your being. They laugh at all of your jokes, cry with you, are happy when you're happy, and want you to enjoy an amazing life. Your unseen friend will always be with you. They will never leave you. They are completely reliable for you to call on and to depend on in all circumstances. Keep it simple, just like this, and let them in.

As you go about your life, proceed with the intention of nurturing the connection and growing the relationship. *Day and night.*

Reclaim your pure heart so that you may enjoy your time here and contribute in ways that really resonate with you. With this new information, you can allow others to journey in their own ways without allowing it to impact you in non-preferred ways. Keep in mind that everyone has unseen friends who love and watch over them! And when the people you love (in your day-to-day world) are in darkness, your very presence can reflect light to them. When you have compassion for yourself, it automatically flows for others because you understand what trying to fulfill unmet needs is all about.

You are loved unconditionally ... no matter what you do or do not do. After you make that connection and get that understanding, you can see that you are only harming yourself when you act out against yourself by abusing yourself or others; you are free to do whatever you want and your unseen friend will still love you. This is unconditional love. *Love without condition.* So if this is the case, why not start thinking about things that you really want to have and create rather than spinning in circles of self-loathing? Create a new habit of thinking and living in ways that make you feel really good about yourself.

This unconditional love is always available to you, and it's unlimited, unconditional and eternal. Imagine that it is there for you, very personal and tailor-made for you. Continue to draw from this ever-replenishing well and use it to fuel yourself as you go about your life.

Once you nurture and cultivate this relationship, you can access that love anytime you need comfort and understanding. Adopt him/her as your friend and protector. And when you realize that you have the ability to access them at anytime, and *allow that love to be your "go to" in trying times as well as triumphant times*, you become free from all the curve balls life may bring. You will *know* that you are truly loved because you will be able to *feel* the love. The separation that exists between your head ("I *should* love myself") and your heart ("I truly *do* love myself") will disappear. Then you can really play!

Offline

Loving qualities like compassion and kindness do indeed exist. If you look around, you can see them.

Think about all of the qualities you associate with love. Now, as you live your life, train yourself to see displays of love in the world.

For example, notice people laughing. See a father holding his daughter's hand as they cross the street. Take note of someone letting you merge into traffic. Acknowledge when a stranger picks up something you dropped and gives it back to you.

Start here and now. Observe acts of love. They're all around you. Notice even just one act of love around you, among those you know and don't know, every day.

ငဒ ငဒ ငဒ

Pep Talk #3

Here are some final thoughts about making lemonade, and here's to your ongoing journey. I celebrate you!

At all times, remember your innocence. It's not possible at this time to know, get or understand your bigger story. You are comprised of so many complex causations and attributes that judging yourself for what you do or do not do is completely inappropriate. You are innocent when it comes to the bigger picture. So the goal is to determine how you can use this understanding now, in the context of your life today, all with the intent of shedding light on the darkness to garner more self-respect. Are you a warrior? Keen on justice? Passionate about children / education? Committed to public service? Want to make previous struggle worth it? Make the world physically beautiful? Where is your passion? And from there, what might be your unique contribution?

It may be very easy for you to identify the shortcomings of others. You may feel that someone in your life could benefit from understanding themselves further. But keep in mind that everyone's experience, circumstances and timing is different. And due to many factors, they may not even be capable of looking at certain things, *ever.* The very thing that you think they could benefit from might be the thing that could derail them. *You never know.* They are living the best life they know how and you can best serve them by addressing your own needs, and utilizing your newly found peace and balance to send them love exactly as they are. They may notice a shift in you and want to know what you're doing. If they ask, share. If not, just love them. It's easier to love someone than to change them. Your ability to identify the shortcomings of others is a directive for *you*, not for *them*. It means that you have the ability to send compassion and understanding their way, so get busy. Remember that you can replenish your love reserves easily and effortlessly in your inner world, so do not hold back on giving love to others. Share as much love, appreciation and admiration for others as possible. Be courageous and let it rip.

You may have been taught that tooting your own horn is immodest, conceited or simply rude. Yet you have wonderful and amazing qualities. Are you supposed to ignore them? Be willing to acknowledge to yourself what you do well. Acknowledge your gifts. When you acknowledge them, it allows you to actually grow them even more, and this can allow you a bigger capacity to serve others. Rely on your ever-growing relationship with your unseen friend for guidance and support on how to use your gifts. Know that there are people who love you that you cannot see, and that circumstances can arise that bring the right people into your life to assist you in sharing your gifts with others.

When you find yourself taking concrete steps to heal your life and maintain your balance, when there are times when you need to take a leap of faith, you will find that you are supported. It's as if you are climbing an invisible ladder. The next step will only appear once you have put your foot forward, trusting that it will be there to support you. Sometimes you have to step out first. It's a silent inner language that you will learn to hear, connect with and move forward with. Stay focused on your healing process and listen to the guidance that whispers to you. You are reconnecting with your discernment skills to be able to know what is loving and kind, and what is not. *Trust yourself!*

As you reconnect with your own trust, keep in mind that you are not perfect. Being perfect implies that there is a limit; that once you arrive at a certain point, there is nowhere else to go. And this is a fallacy. As the universe is always expanding, so are you. Be willing to think in terms of improvement. That you are always getting better and growing and improving. Even if you find yourself revisiting old ideas and non-preferred habits, what may have taken you three years to overcome or understand might now take you three months. Now that's progress!

Also, be gentle with yourself as you become accustomed to working the exercises. Don't feel like you have to force anything. There's more at work than what you can perceive; there is divine influence at work when you embark on your healing journey, so trust yourself and trust the other side assisting on your behalf.

You have certainly encountered roadblocks and made interesting choices, and perhaps you have ended up in places that were far, far away from your intended destination. Consider that those were not interruptions in your path, but part of your path. Think about what you learned from those supposed wrong turns. What strengths did you gain? What insights did you develop? Learning to honor all that you are and have experienced, including the qualities and actions/inactions that cause you concern, may automatically result in a shift in what you believe to be true about yourself. This can afford you a level of peace that may have eluded you your whole life. Once you step into this peace, you will automatically be able to use it as a springboard to create the life you want to live.

Dance and sing. Celebrate who you are! As you pass by a mirror, wink at yourself. You are awesome! You don't have to force your healing process or expect yourself to be further along than you are right now. Your healing process has its own timing, and you are exactly where you need to be. Listen to the way you talk to yourself and shift it to be positive and gentle. You would be kind to an innocent child, wouldn't you? Treat yourself with kindness as well.

Have dialogues with your future self. See your future self in all your glory, having manifested all that you desire. Allow your future self to give you, here and now, words of encouragement and support.

There is nobody else on Earth or in the entire Universe exactly like you. You are absolutely one of a kind. You are special. You are unique. You are important! From the date and hour of your birth, to your DNA, to your personality, to your thoughts and your experiences — all of this is uniquely yours. Embrace your quirks and idiosyncrasies.

They are uniquely yours to acknowledge, understand, and ultimately celebrate. Your quest is for your individuality, your unique expression and desire for love and approval, as well as learning how to operate in this life with joy.

The Dirty Backpack Exercise

And, finally, if ever you find yourself overwhelmed, frustrated, disheartened or confused, take time to go offline — even if for just a moment. Here comes your healing, dear friend:

The Exercise

- Close your eyes and breathe deeply.

- Imagine that you have a backpack on your back.

- Take your anger, your frustration, your sadness, your overwhelm, *all of it*, and load it into the backpack. Keep loading it and loading it. Notice that as you continue to load it up, it gets heavier, dirtier and more disgusting. With each new burden you put into it, it gets dustier and mildewy and smelly and nasty.

- Once you have completely filled it with all of your concerns and considerations, take it off your back.

- As you look in front of you, you see your unseen friend. The one you love and who loves you. Rest assured that they deeply love you. More than you can ever imagine.

- They are smiling at you with arms outstretched. Hand them the dirty backpack. See them receive it with love. They are overjoyed to take it from you and they thank you for giving it to them. They will take it from you to lighten your load.

- Once you see them smile and fade away, give yourself permission to come back into the room.

So here's to you, and here's to your new ability to make lemonade. Challenge yourself to make it as sweet as possible. I applaud you!

Afterword

Your self-healing journey is vibrant, dynamic and alive! This guide is a supplement to all other things you do to live the life of your dreams. Concepts and ideas are plentiful; however, it is the doing and applying of the concepts and ideas that will help you make the shifts you desire. As you apply the concepts and ideas presented here, allow yourself to bend and flow with them.

Every waking minute holds the opportunity to practice at least one of them. *Be patient*! Exercise your heart muscle by having compassion for yourself! Release what is within you that needs a voice. Give yourself permission *to feel*. Share your thoughts and feelings with those you trust. Know that you are loved beyond comprehension. Dance! Celebrate the miracle that YOU are.

About the Author

Janet D. Thomas is a captivating speaker, engaging writer and dynamic workshop leader who practices what she preaches. This imparts to her written and spoken words the power to both inspire and motivate, even heal. And because her message is based upon her per-sonal experience, describing her own transformation literally energizes transformation in those who experience her.

Always seeking for answers, over the course of her life Janet has healed the wounds of childhood sexual abuse and overcome a laundry list of challenges ranging from obesity, eviction and bankruptcy to compulsive lying, clinical depression and divorce. To her, making lemonade is no mere philosophical or psychological proposition; it has been a life-saving strategy.

A lifelong metaphysician and with over 20 years as a trained channel and medium, Janet is a highly effective spiritual coach. Her approach is one of determining how to *do*, rather than how to think. She is a manifester extraordinaire. Because of the intensity, determination, and sheer dedication with which Janet pursues her calling, she is, indeed, a healing soldier.

A native of Southern California, Janet lives, writes and maintains her coaching practice in North Hollywood, California. She is the mother of an adult son, of whom she is very proud.

Janet is available for individual and group sessions,
speaking engagements and seminars.

www.janetdthomas.com